MACHINE GUN PAMPHLET COMPENDIUM

NOTES ON THE EMPLOYMENT OF MACHINE
GUNS IN DESERT WARFARE IN EGYPT — 1916

NOTES AND RULES FOR BARRAGE FIRE
WITH MACHINE GUNS — 1917

INFANTRY MACHINE-GUN COMPANY
TRAINING — 1917

MACHINE-GUN SQUADRON DRILL — 1918

The Naval & Military Press Ltd

Published by the
The Naval & Military Press
in association with the Royal Armouries

Unit 10 Ridgewood Industrial Park,
Uckfield, East Sussex, TN22 5QE
Tel: +44 (0) 1825 749494
Fax: +44 (0) 1825 765701

MILITARY HISTORY AT YOUR FINGERTIPS
www.naval-military-press.com

ONLINE GENEALOGY RESEARCH
www.military-genealogy.com

ONLINE MILITARY CARTOGRAPHY
www.militarymaproom.com

ROYAL
ARMOURIES

The Library & Archives Department at the Royal Armouries Museum, Leeds, specialises in the history and development of armour and weapons from earliest times to the present day. Material relating to the development of artillery and modern fortifications is held at the Royal Armouries Museum, Fort Nelson.

For further information contact:
Royal Armouries Museum, Library, Armouries Drive,
Leeds, West Yorkshire LS10 1LT
Royal Armouries, Library, Fort Nelson, Down End Road, Fareham PO17 6AN

Or visit the Museum's website at
www.armouries.org.uk

In reprinting in facsimile from the original, any imperfections are inevitably reproduced and the quality may fall short of modern type and cartographic standards.

FOR OFFICIAL USE ONLY.

40 / W.O. / 3513

Notes on the Employment

OF

MACHINE GUNS

IN

Desert Warfare in Egypt.

Issued by the General Staff.

December, 1916.

LONDON:
PRINTED FOR HIS MAJESTY'S STATIONERY OFFICE,
BY HARRISON AND SONS, ST. MARTIN'S LANE,
PRINTERS IN ORDINARY TO HIS MAJESTY.

1917.

NOTES ON THE EMPLOYMENT

of

MACHINE GUNS IN DESERT WARFARE.

1. *Control.*—The general experience has been that the control of more than two guns in action is almost always impossible. This bears out the general experience of machine gunners throughout the war.

2. *Stoppages and Action of Sand. Vickers.*—With the Vickers guns the only trouble experienced was that when the guns were mounted in the "Low Position," sand was sucked up into the mechanism through the ejection opening on the underside of the breech casing. This was remedied in some cases by putting a coat under the gun.

Maxim.—A careful consideration of all the reports received from the different units shows that the amount of trouble experienced from stoppages was by no means excessive. In many cases no trouble whatever occurred, and where difficulties did occur they could almost always be traced to two causes :—

(1) the action of sand ; and
(2) the condition of the locks and the lack of spare parts.

As regards the action of sand—as in the case of the Lewis guns—it was obvious that where the trouble from this cause had been foreseen and special precautions had been taken, its ill effects were largely minimised. The following quotation is of interest as bearing out this statement : "No special difficulties were encountered owing to the action of sand in the mechanism, as we were able to keep the guns practically clear of sand by exercising a reasonable amount of care. The guns were examined and cleaned on every possible occasion."

Except when actually in action guns should invariably be kept covered whether on the move or in camp. Bags made from light canvas or any other suitable material can be improvised for this purpose. It should be remembered, however, that guns kept in this way for any length of time need frequent attention ; otherwise they very quickly rust. In emplacements, blinds, where provided, should be kept down whenever possible. Special precautions should be taken whenever the wind is blowing.

The trouble caused by sand can be considered under three headings, viz. :—

(1) its action in the lock,
(2) its action in the feed block, and
(3) its action in the belt.

(1) *The Lock.*—Locks should not be kept dry but covered with a thin film of oil. A wipe over with an oily rag is all that is necessary. The spare lock should be kept in its wallet until actually required. Any loss of time in changing locks is amply repaid by the fresh lock being fit for use.

(2) *The Feed Block.*—The above remarks are equally applicable to feed blocks, special attention being paid, as far as oil is concerned, to the action of the slide.

(3) *The Belts.*—The greatest care should be taken to keep the boxes and belts free from sand. This precaution is specially necessary just after a belt has been fired. What usually happens is that the used portion of the belt is allowed to fall into the sand on one side of the gun, while the box when empty is thrown aside on the other, getting half filled with sand in the process. The belt is then at once refilled and put back into the sandy box. More sand is worked into the belt in the process of refilling. It is from this source that sand finds its way into the feed block causing sluggish feed and trouble with the upper pawls, and hence stoppage in the fourth position.

Too much care cannot be taken in the correct filling and overhauling of belts. The latter duty should be carried out by Nos. 3 and 4 during action. It must be remembered that, however accurately a belt may have been filled before moving off, it is quite possible for a few hours on a pack saddle to render it quite incapable of being fired without stoppages.

Prolonged Stoppages.—These were generally caused by broken cotter pins. This stoppage seems to have occurred to an absolutely inexplicable extent, supposing that the right sized cotter pin was used. It must be remembered that when washers are taken into use the correct size cotter pin must be used with them; this precaution is most essential, otherwise breakages are sure to occur. The length of the connecting rod should be continually tested by the artificers.

In the event of a No. 3 stoppage occurring and of the cover being opened to investigate the cause, the horns of the extractor should always be forced down to remedy this defect. Any attempt to pull them up may lead to an explosion of the cartridge and a resulting accident.

Every effort should be made by Company Commanders to ensure that the sections are as complete as possible in spare parts and particularly in spare locks. In the event of failure to obtain the necessary articles the Company Commanders should report the fact to superior authority.

3. *Transport.*—Pack transport was generally used and appears to have been satisfactory. The weight a horse or mule can carry in heavy sand and the best method of packing to avoid any danger of chafing are matters to which Company Commanders should pay the closest attention.

4. *Ammunition Supply.*—Pack animals supplemented when necessary by camels and limbered wagons appear to have been generally used. Careful arrangements seem to have been made by all Company Commanders to ensure the continuity of their supply, and the results appear to have been successful in all cases. Too much emphasis cannot be laid on the necessity for these arrangements by all M.G. officers.

5. *Combined Sights.*—Combined sights with two guns were used with good results on several occasions. Two instances occur illustrating a right and a wrong method of using this form of fire.

(*a*) Indirect fire with combined sights was used by one section to search the reverse slope of a hill. This proceeding is very sound, and the officer notes in his report that though observation could not be obtained " the Turks came out."

(*b*) Another officer reports that he used combined sights "to obtain the range." Combined sights are useless for this purpose.

6. *Indirect Fire.*—Indirect fire was seldom employed, but opportunities for the use of this method of fire will occur in future. All sections should be instructed in the " Graticule " and " Spirit Level " methods which are very simply and quickly employed in action.

7. *Co-operation between M.G. Companies and Lewis Gun Detachments.*—Co-operation appears to have been attained in several cases, but is not yet sufficiently general. M.G. Company and section officers should give the most careful study to this question both in attack and defence, for it is only by the complete co-operation of all arms that success can be attained. This co-operation should nowhere be closer than between the machine gunners and Lewis gunners, whose methods, up to a certain point, are similar, and therefore make mutual understanding easy.

8. *Overhead Covering Fire.*—Overhead covering fire was used on many occasions, the "Tangent Sight method" being that most commonly employed. All ranks should be instructed in the use of this method, which is of the greatest assistance whenever the control passes from the officer to the No. 1 at the gun. It should

be remembered that the "card and string" method, used in conjunction with it, enables the Section Officer to ensure that his No. 1's are preserving the correct "angle of safety."

9. *Emplacements.*—Great care must be taken in deciding whether overhead cover should be provided or not. It must always be remembered that although such cover is of the greatest value against shrapnel and bullets, it is useless against a direct hit from a heavy shell, and that an emplacement which has been detected, either from the enemy's position or from aircraft reconnaissance, will most certainly be subjected to bombardment and probably destroyed. Several instances of this actually occurred during the operations of last August. Many officers mention in their reports that the scrubby "tumps," which are common in some localities, can easily and quickly be converted into emplacements in which guns are quite indistinguishable, and they say that guns which have been brought forward to a "position of readiness" are far safer when kept in these than when on the reverse slopes of hills or in valleys, both of which were always heavily shelled. Light overhead cover on which pieces of scrub were planted would in these cases be of great protection against hostile aircraft reconnaissance. Great care must be taken in cases where emplacements are furnished with overhead cover that the latter is high enough for the cover to be lifted and the lock and feed-block removed if necessary. This should always be tested *at once* on taking over emplacements from other troops.

Loopholes should be blinded when the gun is not actually in use. Care must be taken that they are of sufficient size not to restrict the field of fire of the guns.

10. *Horsemanship.*—Since rapid reconnaissance is essential in all machine gun tactics, officers commanding companies should ensure that all their section officers are sufficiently expert horsemen to enable them to make full use of the chargers at their disposal.

11. *Spare Barrels.*—Several extemporised methods of carrying the spare barrel were observed. It is absolutely necessary that some dust-proof covering or box should be provided for this article when pack transport is employed.

12. *Sledges.*—Frequent attention is drawn in officers' reports to the long distances which guns had to be carried owing to the lack of cover for transport animals. It is thought that some light form of sledge might be of use in desert warfare, and experiments in this direction might well be worth undertaking.

13. *Fire.*—An idea appears to have arisen in some quarters that the machine gun is best adapted for enfilade fire, the Lewis gun

for direct fire. The second part of the theory is entirely false. Machine guns of whatever description should always attempt to obtain oblique or when possible enfilade fire for which they are peculiarly adapted. The mistake may perhaps have arisen from the fact that the arrangement of guns advocated for the defence of a position is that the machine guns should form the "Belt of Fire" while the Lewis guns cover avenues of approach which are, from the conformation of the ground, protected from the fire of the former. This often leads to the Lewis guns having to be employed to bring a direct fire to bear down such approaches, but this is always a matter of necessity and not of choice.

14. *Command.*—As some doubts seem still to exist on the matter the following decision as regards the command of machine gun sections may be of help to M.G. Officers and others :—" M.G. Sections detached from their company and ordered to co-operate with any body of troops are under the orders of the Officer Commanding those troops, and the Company Commander cannot move or take away any such sections without the permission of that officer or a direct order from the Brigadier. The M.G. Company Commander may give his advice as to the use or disposition of such sections, but the responsibility as to whether or not he takes that advice rests with the Commander of the troops. Sections held in reserve or detailed for special duties are under the orders of the M.G. Company Commander."

OFFICIAL COPY.

[*Crown Copyright Reserved.*]

$\frac{40}{\frac{W.O.}{3330}}$

INFANTRY MACHINE-GUN COMPANY TRAINING.
(*Provisional.*)

1917.

To be read in conjunction with Infantry Training and Musketry Regulations.

ISSUED BY THE GENERAL STAFF.

LONDON:
PUBLISHED BY HIS MAJESTY'S STATIONERY OFFICE.

To be purchased through any Bookseller or directly from
H.M. STATIONERY OFFICE at the following addresses:
IMPERIAL HOUSE, KINGSWAY, LONDON, W.C., and 28, ABINGDON STREET, LONDON, S.W.;
37, PETER STREET, MANCHESTER; 1, ST. ANDREW'S CRESCENT, CARDIFF;
23, FORTH STREET, EDINBURGH;
or from E. PONSONBY, LTD., 116, GRAFTON STREET, DUBLIN;
or from the Agencies in the British Colonies and Dependencies,
the United States of America and other Foreign Countries of
T. FISHER UNWIN, LTD., LONDON, W.C.

1917.

Price Sixpence Net.

PREFACE.

This Manual is issued by command of the Army Council.

WAR OFFICE,
 22nd February, 1917.

CONTENTS.

CHAPTER I.
ORGANIZATION AND DEFINITIONS.

SEC.		PAGE.
1. Organization	...	6
2. Definitions	...	6

CHAPTER II.
PRINCIPLES AND SYSTEM OF TRAINING.

3. General instructions	...	8
4. Annual training	...	8
5. Elementary training	...	9

CHAPTER III.
SECTION AND COMPANY DRILL.

SECTION DRILL.

6. General Rules	...	9

COMPANY DRILL.

7. General rules	...	10
8. A company in line moving to a flank in column of route, "Action expected"	...	10
9. A company in line moving to a flank in column of route, "Action not expected"	...	11
10. A company in line advancing in column of sections	...	12
11. A company in column of sections forming line in the same direction	...	12

CHAPTER III—continued.

SEC.		PAGE.
12.	A company in column of route, "Action not expected," forming line facing a flank	13
13.	A company in column of route, "Action expected" forming line facing a flank	13
14.	A company in column of route, "Action expected," forming line in the same direction	14
15.	A company in column of route, "Action not expected," forming line in the same direction	14

CHAPTER IV.
MACHINE GUN DRILL.

16.	Allocation of duties	15
17.	Elementary drill	17
18.	Combined drill	26
19.	Auxiliary mounting drill	26
20.	Rough ground drill	30
21.	Trench drill	31
22.	Section tactical exercises	36

CHAPTER V.
FIRE DIRECTION.

23.	General remarks	39
24.	Traversing fire	39
25.	Searching fire	40
26.	Combined sights	41
27.	Overhead fire	43
28.	Indirect fire	45
29.	Night firing	56
30.	Indirect overhead fire	58
31.	Searching reverse slopes	63

CHAPTER VI.
MACHINE GUNS IN BATTLE.

SEC.		PAGE.
32.	Introductory	65
33.	Characteristics of machine-guns and Lewis guns compared	66
34.	The employment of Lewis guns	67
35.	The tactical handling of infantry machine-guns	68
36.	Machine-guns in the attack	71
37.	Machine-guns in the defence	74
38.	Machine-guns with an advanced guard	76
39.	Machine-guns with a rear guard	76
40.	Village fighting	77
41.	Occupation of various positions	78
42.	Signals	79

APPENDIX A.

			PAGE
Table	I.	Tangent elevation, angles of descent, &c.	
Table	IIA.	Trajectory table	80
Table	IIB.	Trajectory table for negative quadrant angles	81
Table	IIIA.	Quadrant angle—Target ABOVE gun	82
Table	IIIB.	Quadrant angle—Target BELOW gun	83
Table	IV.	Wind allowances	84
Table	V.	Allowances for atmospheric influences	85
Table	VI.	Time of flight	86
Table	VII.	Searching reverse slopes	87

APPENDIX B.

Indirect overhead fire sheet 88

PLATES.

CHAPTER I.

ORGANIZATION AND DEFINITIONS.

1. *Organization.*

1. A machine-gun company consists of:—

> Headquarters.
> Sections, each of 4 guns.

The guns may be either Vickers or Maxim, but all the guns of the same company will be of the same pattern.

2. A machine-gun company is commanded by a major or captain, with a captain or lieutenant as second in command.

Each section is divided into two sub-sections, each commanded by a subaltern with a serjeant as second in command. The senior of the two subalterns also commands the section.

3. The machine guns of a section are carried in 2 limbered G.S. wagons. Each section has also 1 limbered G.S. wagon for ammunition.

4. Further details as to personnel and vehicles are given in War Establishments.

2. *Definitions.*

The following definitions are added to those given in Infantry Training :—

Band of fire.—When a machine gun is fired so that the cone of fire is directed on a fixed aiming mark, while the gun is so sighted that the first catch is at the muzzle and the cone never rises above the height of a man, a *band of fire* is formed in the space between the first catch and the first graze. (See Plate XVII.)

For practical purposes on flat ground, the trajectory limits the length of the band to 600 yards.

Detachment.—(In a machine-gun company.) The number of men detailed for the service of 1 gun. Each detachment is numbered from 1 to 6, permanent duties being allotted to each number. (See Sections 16 and 17.)

Fighting limbers.—Those limbers detailed to carry the guns, tripods and first supply of ammunition.

In action.—A machine gun is said to be "in action" when it is mounted, loaded and laid, but is not necessarily firing.

Indirect fire.—Fire directed at an object or area of ground which is invisible from the gun position.

Laying.—The process of elevating and traversing a gun till its axis is made to point in any given direction. On completion of this process the gun is said to be *laid*.

Machine gun.—A gun of the Vickers or Maxim type. Lewis guns are not included in the term *Machine gun*.

Position of readiness.—A position in which guns and personnel are assembled preparatory to coming into action.

Ranges, terms applied to.—These are the same for machine guns as for the rifle.

Screen of fire.—If machine guns are sited on any given defensive line so that no portion of the ground in front of that line is unswept by at least one band of fire, that front is said to be protected by a *screen of fire.* (See Plate XVIII.)

CHAPTER II.

PRINCIPLES AND SYSTEM OF TRAINING.

3. *General Instructions.*

The principles and system of training laid down in Infantry Training, Chapter I, apply to the training of the personnel of machine-gun companies.

4. *Annual training.*

1. The details given in Infantry Training, Section 8, require modification to suit the new organization of machine-gun companies.

2. (*a*) The establishment given in para. 1 of the above quoted Section has been superseded.

   (*b*) Para. 2. There will be no brigade machine-gun officer, but when necessary the commander of the machine-gun company attached to the brigade will act as such.

3. Machine-gun companies will, if available, be practised in field operations with infantry battalions, sections being also

occasionally detailed to co-operate with companies of infantry during their training.

5. *Elementary training.*

The personnel of machine-gun companies are trained as infantry soldiers in squad drill, as laid down in Infantry Training, before being instructed in the special formations necessary for machine-gun companies which are given in Chapter III of this manual.

CHAPTER III.

SECTION AND COMPANY DRILL.

Section Drill.

6. *General Rules.*

1. A section will be exercised in all the movements of squad drill, the word section being substituted for squad.

2. The rules laid down in Infantry Training, Chapter III, for section and platoon drill will apply. It must be remembered that a machine-gun section corresponds to a platoon, and a sub-section to an infantry section.

3. The normal positions of the units of a machine-gun section formed up on parade for inspection are given in Plate I, but a section parading by itself for inspection will fall in with one pace interval between sub-sections.

COMPANY DRILL.

7. *General Rules.*

1. The object of and rules for company drill of a machine-gun company are the same as laid down in Infantry Training, Chapter IV, for an infantry company, with the provisos laid down in Section 6 (2) of this manual.

2. The normal positions of the units of a machine-gun company in line and in column of route, are given in Plates I, II and III.

3. The detail of some special movements is given in the following sections.

* 8. *A company in line moving to a flank in column of route, " Action expected."*

Move to the Right (or Left) in Column of Route. No. Section Leading.

1. The company commander, company serjeant-major and signallers will take post on the flank nearest the direction of march.

2. The section commanders will give the command *No. — Section, Form-Fours, Right* (or *Left*), *Quick—March*, on which the gun limber nearest the flank of march will wheel into column of route, followed by its sub-section and in succession by the remaining gun limbers and sub-sections in that order.

---

* In this and the following sections the title of the section or of the movement is shown in *italics*, and is followed in the next line by the caution or executive word of command in **thick type**. The body of the section contains the detail. Cautions or words of command referred to in the detail are in *italics*.

3. The ammunition limbers will follow the rear section in the same order as their sections. They will be followed by the headquarters limber, water cart, cook's cart, and train transport in rear in that order.

9. *A company in line moving to a flank in column of route, "Action not expected."*

Move to the Right (or Left) in Column of Route, Detachments Leading ; Sections, Form—Fours, Right (or Left).

1. The company serjeant-major and signallers will take post at the head of the column.

Quick—March.

1. The men of the detachments will act as in squad drill.

2. When the rear of the detachments are clear, the sub-section officer of the leading section will place himself at the head of the gun limber nearest the direction of march and give the command *No. — Section, Walk— March.* This limber will be followed by the other gun limber, while the No. 3 limber waits till the gun limbers of the remaining sections have passed. The remaining sub-section commanders will act in a like manner in succession.

3. The ammunition limbers, headquarters' limber, water cart, cook's cart, and train transport will follow in that order in rear, supervised by the second in command and the transport serjeant, who will ride in rear of the column.

4. The corporals and other details, as shown in Plate II, will act as brakesmen to the fighting limbers and other vehicles respectively.

10. *A company in line advancing in column of sections.*

Advance in Column of Sections from the Right (or Left).

1. The company serjeant-major and signallers will take post in front of the section commander on the right (or left) of the line, distances as in Plate I.

2. No. 1 section commander will give the command *No. 1 Section, by the Right. Quick—March.* The remaining section commanders in succession will give the command *No. — Section, Quick—March*, on which they will lead their sections into their places in column in rear of the preceding section.

3. The ammunition limbers will take post in rear of the last section, the limber nearest the flank of direction leading followed by the headquarters' limber, water cart, cook's cart, and train transport.

11. *A company in column of sections forming line in the same direction.*

At the Halt, on the Left (or Right), Form Line, Remainder Left (or Right)—Incline.

1. The leading section commander will give the command *No. — Section, Halt.* The remaining sections will incline as ordered, when each section is immediately in rear of its position in line, it will receive from its commander, *Left (or Right) Incline*, and, when on alignment, *Halt*. The section commander will, if necessary, give the command *Right* (or

Left) *Dress*, on which the whole will take up their dressing by the flank of direction.

2. The company serjeant-major, signallers, ammunition limbers, water cart, &c., will move to their places in line during the movement.

3 This movement will always be done at the halt.

12. *A company in column of route, " Action not expected," forming line facing a flank.*

At the Halt, Line to the Left (or Right), Company Halt, Left (or Right) Turn.

1. The men of the detachments will act as in squad drill.

2. The sub-section officers and the transport serjeant will lead their wagons to their places in line during the movement, and when the movement is completed will take up their places in line.

3. The company serjeant-major, signallers, servants, cooks, &c., will take up their places in line during the movement.

13. *A company in column of route, " Action expected," forming line facing a flank.*

At the Halt, facing Left (or Right), Form Line.

The leading gun limber will wheel in the named direction and halt, followed by the remaining gun limbers, which will wheel and halt in succession as they arrive at the correct interval. They will be followed by their respective sub-sections, which will be led to their places in line by their sub-section serjeants, who will give the command *Halt, Left* (or *Right*) *Turn*.

2. The company serjeant-major, signallers, ammunition limbers, headquarters' limber, water-cart, cook's cart, and train transport will move to their places in line during the movement.

14. *A company in column of route, " Action expected," forming line in the same direction.*

At the Halt, on the Left (or Right), Form Line.

The leading gun limber will halt, the remainder disengaging to the left (or right) and taking up their places in line. As the gun limbers arrive at their places, their respective sub-sections will disengage by the right. On reaching the correct distance in front of the gun limbers, each sub-section serjeant will give the command *At the Halt, on the Left* (or *Right*), *Form Sub-section.*

2. The company serjeant-major, signallers, ammunition limbers, headquarters' limber, water-cart, &c., will move to their places in line during the movement.

15. *A company in column of route, " Action not expected," forming line in the same direction.*

At the Halt, on the Left (or Right), Form—Company.

1. The men of the detachments will act as in squad drill.

2. The gun limbers will be led to their places in line by their respective sub-section officers.

3. The company serjeant-major, signallers, cooks, servants, &c., ammunition limbers, headquarters' limber, water-cart, cook's cart, and train transport will move to their places in line during the movement.

CHAPTER IV.

MACHINE GUN DRILL.

Note.—The following Sections 16 and 17 are substituted for Sections 102 and 103 respectively in Infantry Training, Chapter VII. Additional Sections, 18 to 22, are added for more advanced training. In order that training may be progressive the sequence of these sections should be adhered to.

16. *Allocation of duties.*

1. The duties of the section commander are to command the section in accordance with his orders and the tactical situation, to select gun positions, to observe and to control fire generally, to regulate the ammunition supply, and to give instructions regarding the movements of limbered wagons.

2. The duties of the sub-section officer are to assist the section commander and to act as second in command of the section. He should be ready to replace the section commander should the latter become a casualty. Normally he will command one sub-section in action and supervise the transport of his section in quarters and on the line of march.

3. The duty of the serjeant is to supervise guns coming into action as the section officer may direct. He must be prepared to take command of the section in the event of both the officers becoming casualties. He is responsible for replacing casualties among the gun numbers when they occur.

4. The corporal is responsible generally for the packing and contents of the gun limber. On the line of march he marches behind it and works the brake as required. On

the order to unpack he will superintend the unpacking, and take command in the absence of the section officer or serjeant. He will have the spare parts box handy, supervise the ammunition supply and filling of belts, direct the gun limber as required, superintend the filling of sandbags and watch for signals from the section officer. He will be prepared to take the place of the serjeant should he become a casualty.

5. The following are the duties of the various numbers :—

No. 1 is the firer. He will personally clean and look after his gun and ensure that the mechanism is working smoothly. On going into action he will carry the Mark IV tripod and place it in a suitable position and assist No. 2 in mounting the gun. He repeats all orders received, observes his own fire when possible, and makes the necessary alterations of elevation and direction.

No. 2 assists No. 1 at the gun, carries the gun into action when No. 1 is carrying the tripod, and mounts it with the assistance of No. 1.

On going into action he will secure the tube of the condenser to the gun, and take the first aid case. In action he will attend to the feeding of the gun, watch for signals from the section or company officer, and generally assist No. 1.

No. 3 is responsible for keeping the gun supplied with ammunition; seeing that the condenser (half-filled with water) reaches the gun position before there is any chance of the water in barrel casing boiling; and carrying out minor repairs whilst the gun is in action.

No. 4 assists No. 3 in his duties. He is responsible for keeping No. 3 supplied with ammunition, water, and spare parts from the spare parts box as required.

Nos. 5 and 6 are spare men. These numbers and the scout and range-taker, if detailed to the section, act according to the orders of the section or sub-section officer.

6. Section officers will ensure that each man of the section is thoroughly trained in the duties of each "number." A system of "changing round" will be arranged, so that every man will perform the several duties of the section in turn.

17. *Elementary drill.*

Note.—Elementary drill consists of the following :—

(*a*) Mounting the gun.
(*b*) Loading.
(*c*) Sight-setting and laying.
(*d*) Unloading.
(*e*) Dismounting the gun.
(*f*) Coming into action.
(*g*) Coming out of action.
(*h*) Tap traversing and vertical searching.
(*i*) Use of condenser tube and bag with water.
(*j*) Elementary drill with gun mounted in lowest position.

1. The guns of a sub-section, with tripods and ammunition boxes, will be placed on the ground, muzzles to the front and in line, legs to the rear, and clamps sufficiently tight to prevent the legs from hanging loose when the tripod is lifted off the ground; the traversing clamp should be sufficiently loose to enable the gun to be deflected by a sharp tap with the hand on the rear cross-piece; guns on the right, ammunition boxes three paces in rear of the guns. The guns should be a convenient distance apart, but not closer than eight paces.

2. On the command *Fall in*, the sub-section will fall in in two ranks, five paces in front of the interval between the

two guns, the serjeant on the left of the front rank, covered by the corporal in the rear rank. The front rank will provide the right gun detachment, the rear rank the left gun detachment.

On the command *Number*, the sub-section will number from right to left.

On the command *Take Post*, detachments turn outwards and double to their respective guns (the serjeant and the corporal on the outer flank, where they can superintend). Nos. 1 and 2 fall in on the left of the tripod and right of the gun respectively, No. 3 on the left of the ammunition box. If the ground is suitable, these numbers should lie down.

Nos. 4, 5, 6 should take up positions as directed by the instructor.

3. Before commencing drill, each " number " will examine the gun and equipment as follows:

No. 1 will examine the tripod and see that—
- (a) The legs are closely folded and clamped.
- (b) The traversing clamp is *sticky*.
- (c) The pins are in and turned down.
- (d) The elevating screws are exposed the same amount.

No. 2 will examine the gun, and see that—
- (a) The lock is in and the lockspring is released.
- (b) The sliding shutter is closed (in the Vickers gun).
- (c) The feed block is in and the front cover catch of the Vickers gun turned down.
- (d) The T fixing-pin is screwed up and vertical (Vickers gun).
- (e) The cork plug is in.
- (f) The slide of the tangent sight is adjusted to 600 yards.

(g) The auxiliary mounting is correctly fixed and in working order.

No. 3 will examine the belt and see that—

(a) The cartridges are correctly placed.

(b) The belt is packed correctly in the box and the lid fastened.

Nos. 2 and 3 will report to No. 1 when they are satisfied that all is correct.

4. In each stage of the drill the correct method will first be demonstrated by the instructor, and will then be practised by each member of the team before proceeding to the next stage. During drill, the spare numbers will be brought up near the gun to watch and listen to the criticism. No. 1 will always repeat the words of command loudly and clearly.

5. *Mounting the gun.*—A machine-gun instructional target or landscape target will be placed about 25 yards from the guns. The instructor will point out a place for the guns to be mounted, not more than 5 yards from where they are lying. He will then give the command *Mount Gun.*

No. 1 picks up the tripod, carries it to the spot ordered, and places it in position. In adjusting the tripod he must ensure that the socket is upright and that the legs are clamped tight. He must learn by experience **the adjustment that suits him best for the position ordered and for the nature of the ground, so that he will not be cramped when firing and will not have to alter the tripod after the gun has been mounted.**

As soon as the tripod is nearly in position, No. 2 picks up the gun (with Vickers gun pushes the sliding shutter to the rear), and carries it to the right side of the tripod, holding the rear cross-piece with the left hand, with the gun muzzle to the rear under the right arm. He then kneels on the left knee, facing the tripod, and, supporting the gun on the right knee, places it on the tripod, drives in and turns down the cross-head joint pin, and removes the cork plug from the steam escape hole. No 1 fixes the elevating joint pin, and directs the gun towards the mark. Meanwhile, No. 2 lies down and places the ammunition box in position.

No. 2 should time his advance so as to reach the tripod at the moment its adjustment is completed.

When No. 3 sees that the gun is nearly mounted, he carries the ammunition box forward and places it within reach of No. 2. The ammunition must be at hand directly No. 2 is ready for it. No. 3 then retires to a position not immediately in rear of the gun. (Standard time—20 seconds.)

6. *Loading.*—On the command *Load*, No. 1 pulls the crank handle on to the roller (**Maxim**—Turns the crank handle on to the buffer spring). No. 2 passes the tag of the belt through the feed block. No. 1 with his left hand pulls the belt straight through to the left front as far as it will go and releases the crank handle. Relaxing the strain on the belt, No. 1 pulls the crank handle on to the roller (**Maxim**— turns the crank handle on to the buffer spring), pulls the belt to the left front and releases the crank handle. Each motion should be clean and distinct. (Standard time—5 seconds.)

The gun is now loaded and ready to fire.

7. *Sight setting.*—For ranges not exceeding 500 yards the fixed sight will be ordered, except when firing at a very small target, when orders will be given as in the case of ranges over 500 yards.

Sec. 17.]

For ranges over 500 yards, on the command (*Range*), *e.g.* "*900*," No. 1 raises the tangent sight, repeats the order for his own gun, and adjusts the slide to the elevation required for the distance ordered.

8. *Laying.*—On the command *At* _____ (naming the aiming mark), No. 2 adjusts the traversing clamp if told to do so by No. 1, and No. 1 lays the gun, maintaining the same pressure on the handles while laying as he would when firing.

When the gun is laid, No. 1 raises the automatic safety catch with the forefinger, and prepares to fire. When No. 1 is ready, No. 2 holds out his left hand and arm horizontally.

9. As proficiency increases, the pause between naming the range and the aiming mark should be slight. (Standard time for sight setting and laying—12 seconds; taken from the time the range is ordered until No. 2 holds out his hand.)

10. On the command or signal *Fire*, No. 1 presses the thumbpiece or double button.

11. On the command or signal *Cease Fire*, No. 1 releases the pressure on the thumbpiece or double button, and remains steady.

12. The points for criticism when the gun is mounted should follow a definite sequence.

(*a*) **Tripod.**
  i. Position of legs with reference to the ground.
  ii. Clamps of leg tight.
  iii. Socket upright.
  iv. Traversing clamp *sticky*.
  v. All pins in and turned down.
  vi. Elevating screws equidistant.
  vii. Rear leg in prolongation of line of sight to the target.

(b) **Gun.**
   i. Muzzle towards the target.
   ii. Cork plug out.
   iii. Shutter back.
   iv. Belt box in line with the feed block.
   v. No. 1 with holding taken and elbows supported on thighs.
   vi. No. 2 in position.
   vii. Gun fairly level.
   viii. Tangent sight set to 600 yards.

(c) The following points should also be noted:—
   i. Loading; the clearness of loading must be insisted on.
   ii. Accuracy of sight testing.
   iii. Absolute accuracy of aim.
   iv. Firing; that on the order or signal being given, to open fire, the double button or thumb-piece is immediately pressed, without disturbing the laying.

13. *Unloading.*—On the command *Unload*, No. 1 lowers the tangent sight, if it has been raised, and leaves the sight as last adjusted; he pulls the crank handle twice in succession on to the roller, letting it fly back each time on to the check lever, and finally depresses the lower pawls (**Maxim**.—He turns the crank handle twice in succession on to the buffer spring, letting it fly back each time on to the check lever); while No. 2 withdraws the belt and packs it in the box; this must be done correctly, and the lid closed and fastened; No. 1 releases the lock spring by pressing the double button, or thumb-piece. (Standard time—5 seconds.)

14. *Dismounting the gun.*—On the command *Dismount Gun*, No. 1 removes the elevating and cross-head joint pins.

No. 2 passes the ammunition box to No. 3, replaces the cork plug when the condenser is not in use, removes the gun as in mounting, and replaces it in its original position in rear. On reaching this position, he closes the sliding shutter (Vickers), and readjusts the tangent sight to 600 if previously altered.

No. 1 carries back the tripod, replaces the cross-head and elevating joint pins, taking care that they are turned down, and then folds and clamps the legs. (Standard time—15 seconds.)

15. *Coming into action.*—As proficiency increases, the gunners should be exercised in performing all the movements required to bring the gun into action.

On the command or signal *Action* (followed by range and aiming mark) the gunners will, from the positions described in para. 2, combine all the foregoing details of mounting, loading and laying the gun, No. 2 signifying when No. 1 is "ready" to fire. (Standard time—35 seconds.)

16. *Coming out of action.*—On the command or signal *Out of Action*, the gun will be unloaded without withdrawing the belt from the feed block. No. 1 will seize the rear leg and rapidly withdraw the gun and tripod under cover or to the original position, with the least possible exposure. No. 2 similarly will withdraw the ammunition box. The gun will then be dismounted in the usual manner. If the cover is some distance away, Nos. 1 and 2 will carry the gun, tripod and belt box in the most convenient manner to cover.

17. *Tap traversing.*—Frequent instruction will be given in traversing fire. The firer must first ensure that the traversing clamp is just sufficiently loose to enable the gun to be

deflected by means of a sharp tap with the hand on the rear crosspiece. Each man must learn by experience the exact degree of clamping he requires, and before firing he should ensure that the clamp is correctly adjusted to suit himself.

Traversing fire is applied by means of a series of groups fired at intervals within certain limits indicated by such figures on the machine gun instructional target as may be ordered by the instructor.

The procedure for horizontal traversing is as follows:— The instructor having described the figures between which fire is to be directed, will give the command *Traversing* followed by the signal to fire. The firer will lay the gun on the flank figure named and press the button, then tap the gun approximately to the centre of the interval to the next figure, again press the button, then tap and so on until the limit ordered has been reached. The firer should be taught to fire groups of about eight rounds by maintaining pressure on the button for about one second at each group. By this method he will learn to tap the gun with the necessary force in order to avoid firing more than one group at the same place, and also to avoid leaving gaps in the line he is traversing. (Standard time—2 seconds for each completed series, *i.e.*, a group and completed traverse.)

As proficiency increases, instruction should be given in diagonal traversing. In this case the target will be three bands each with three figures as for horizontal traversing. The bands will be joined so that each of the outer bands is in the same vertical plane as the centre band and forms an angle of 120 degrees with it.

In this case the firer is taught to combine the use of the elevating wheel with tapping for deflection, the same principles being applied as in horizontal traversing. Instruction should be afforded in traversing from right to left as well as from left to right.

During instruction, fire should be stopped at least twice in order to check the laying and also to measure the distance traversed. By comparing the distance traversed with the groups fired, an estimate can be made as to the value of the traversing fired. For example:—Traversing fire is ordered from the first to the sixth figure; fire is stopped after the fourth group. If the traverse had been correctly carried out, the gun should be laid on the interval between the second and third figures. (Standard time—3 seconds for each completed group and traverse.)

18. *Swinging Traverse.*—Against dense targets at close range, the normal method of traversing is too slow, and fire is unnecessarily concentrated. The " Swinging Traverse " will therefore be employed for this purpose. This consists of rapidly traversing a given line with the traversing clamp loose, the limit and speed of traverse being controlled by the action of the gunner.

Elementary instruction in " Swinging Traverse " will be given on the machine gun instructional target. The gunner will be trained to traverse evenly and smoothly the breadth of the target from outside figure to outside figure in about five seconds.

As proficiency is attained, practice will be afforded in traversing various types of targets which are suitable for this method of fire.

18. *Combined drill.*

Instruction in machine-gun signals (see Infantry Training, Section 164) must be given before combined drill is commenced, and these signals should henceforth be used whenever possible.

Combined drill is best carried out with four or more guns. Condensers will always be attached and bags filled. Barrel casings will also be filled. Competition between detachments should be encouraged with a view to increasing proficiency in elementary drill. The following subjects are taught during combined drill :—

(a) The execution and delivery of fire orders.
(b) The use of combined sights.
(c) Indication and recognition of targets.
(d) Immediate action.
(e) The replacement of breakages.
(f) Casualties.

The instructor should take times, correct mistakes, and carefully note the performance of each detail. When combined drill is carried on out of doors in fine weather, all numbers should lie down, 3 and 4 forming a short chain, and the remainder representing reserves in the rear.

19. *Auxiliary mounting drill.*

1. The auxiliary (light) mounting is not intended to replace the Mark IV tripod. The gun can be placed on the Mark IV tripod without removing the light mounting.

It is intended for use in :—

(a) The firing line.
(b) Rapid advances.

(c) Trench to trench rushes.
(d) Fighting in captured trenches when hurried changes of position are essential, &c.
(e) Trench fighting, when the gun has to be fired hurriedly from a position other than the battle emplacement, or when the Mark IV tripod has been destroyed.

The gun can be carried by either one or two men, as desired. The leather straps, one on the rear cross-piece and one on the front clip band, enable Nos. 1 and 2 to carry the gun between them. They should move in single file, thus concealing the gun from the front. In this way the fact that a machine-gun is being brought up will be more easily concealed from the enemy.

When in action in the open with the light mounting, No. 1 should lie on his back, with his legs to the left of the tripod, No. 2 being on his right-hand side, supporting the firer's back and neck with his legs. (See Plate VII.)

2. When it is desired to have the gun carried by one man, Nos. 1 and 2 should move extended to two or three paces, but conforming as far as possible to neighbouring infantry extensions, No. 1 carrying the gun and No. 2 two or more boxes of ammunition and first aid case.

3. The following method will be taught in addition to other methods which may be suitable on special occasions. The gun will be carried vertically on the right-hand side, muzzle upwards, the right hand grasping the rear leather band, back of the hand to the front, and taking all the weight; the left hand steadying the muzzle end by means of the light mounting clip.

The method of carrying the gun on the shoulder leads to exposure, and is unsuitable in trenches or when in close contact with the enemy.

The condenser tube will be attached throughout.

4. (a) For drill purposes about 3 seconds after No. 1 has opened fire he should pull the crank handle on to the roller, thus allowing the short length of belt to be pulled through the feed block and the web belt inserted.

(b) The fixed sight is invariably used in light mounting work; consequently the tangent sight will not be raised.

(c) Stoppages should be practised.

(d) When this drill is carried out on rough ground the necessary precautions for concealment will be observed when bringing the gun into and out of action.

5. *Drill with "Two-Man Load."*—The gun, with light mounting attached, legs closed and engaged in the clip, will be placed on the ground 20 yards in the rear of the selected position upon which the gun is to be brought into action.

The muzzle of the gun will be placed to the front.

Nos. 1 and 2, each with an ammunition belt box containing a few dummy cartridges at the end of the belt, will assume the prone position, No. 1 behind the rear cross-piece, No. 2 on the right of the gun. No. 2 will have also a short length of belt with two dummy cartridges in its leading end, and the first aid case.

The condenser bag will not be carried.

6. On the caution *Prepare to Advance.*— No. 1 will:—

(a) Pull back the sliding shutter.

(b) Perform the first half of the loading motion.

(c) Throw the short length of belt over the feed block to the left.
(d) Release the lock spring.
(e) Turn the gun on its left-hand side.

No. 2 will :—

(a) Insert the short length of belt in the feed block.
(b) See that the front leather strap is to the top.
(c) Open the tripod legs after (e).

7. On the command *Action*.—The numbers spring to their feet seizing the appropriate straps, and, each carrying a belt box in the disengaged hand, will move rapidly to the position selected. No. 1 has the strap in his right hand, No. 2 in his left hand.

8. On arrival at the position, No. 1 will call out *Action* and :—

(a) Steady the tripod and lie down, placing the belt box in a convenient position for No. 2.
(b) Throw the short length of belt over to the right and complete the loading motions.
(c) Adjust the rear leather strap if necessary.
(d) Open fire.

No. 2 will :—

(a) Turn down the front leather strap.
(b) Lie down and support No. 1.
(c) Open the belt box and hold a new belt ready.

9. On the caution *Prepare to Advance*, preceded by the command *Cease Fire*.—No. 1 will unload ; No. 2 removes the web belt and inserts the short length of belt, if there has been time to replace it.

10. On the command *Out of Action.*—The gun will be unloaded without removing the belt from the feed block and will be withdrawn until cover is reached, when No. 1 will:—

(a) Depress the pawls and release the lockspring.
(b) Close the sliding shutter.

No. 2 will:—

(a) Pack away the belts.
(b) Adjust the front strap.

Both will then jump up and retire, carrying the boxes and gun.

11. *Drill with " Single Load."*—As for drill with the two-man load, except that No. 2 will carry both belt boxes.

12. On the caution *Prepare to Advance.*—The same procedure will be followed as for the two-man load, except that No. 2 should see that the front strap is at the *bottom.*

13. On the command *Action.*—As for the two-man load, except that No. 1 carries the gun alone; No. 2 the belt boxes. In moving forward, No. 2 should extend to the right, and close in again on No. 1 on nearing the position.

The remainder of the drill follows the same lines as for the two-man load.

20. *Rough ground drill.*

1. The gun will be mounted throughout on a steep slope, for firing in each of the following directions in turn:—

(a) Down.
(b) Up.
(c) Horizontally to the right.
(d) Horizontally to the left.

Nos. 1, 2, and 3 with the gun, tripod, and ammunition box, and 4 with water-bag (full) and another box of ammunition, will be in a position of readiness not more than 10 yards from the selected position. The instructor having marked the position and pointed it out, the gun numbers, on receipt of a target and range, will, on the order *Action,* mount, load, and lay the gun on the target indicated. The same procedure will be followed for each of the four positions.

2. The following points are important:—
   (a) Correct setting up of the tripod, the rear leg always downhill.
   (b) The positions adopted by Nos. 1 and 2 (as regards fire effect, exposure and comfort).
   (c) The position of the ammunition box to ensure correct feed.
   (d) The position of No. 3 (minimum exposure with facility for supply).
   (e) The position of No. 4.
   (f) The gun must be properly in action, and all details of elementary training must be observed.

21. *Trench drill.*

1. The object of trench drill is to practise:—
   (a) Posting and relieving sentries and Nos. 1.
   (b) Relieving detachments.
   (c) Action in trenches.
   (d) Preparing to advance and coming into action.
   (e) Quick change to an alternative position.

All the above should be practised on the barrack square before drill takes place in the trenches.

2. *Posting and relief of sentries and Nos. 1.*—The principles involved are identical with those of posting and relief of an infantry sentry on guard or outpost duty.

3. At a gun position in trenches:—
   (a) *By day* only one number need be on duty at the gun position, and he will be the sentry.
   (b) *By night* two men will always be on duty; one being the sentry, who is keeping a look-out, and the second being the No. 1 for the term of duty. The latter is actually at the gun, and may sit down, but must be awake.

4. A gun number (if by night, usually the last number on gun duty) will be posted as a sentry—by day with a periscope, or at a loophole if no periscope is available; by night, looking over the parapet. He will be acquainted with the position of all emplacements allotted to his gun, and will have a thorough knowledge of the following:—
   (a) The section of the ground covered by the gun which it is his duty to watch.
   (b) Points shown on the range card.
   (c) Special orders for his gun position during his relief. These may include action as regards patrols, wiring parties, &c.
   (d) Standing orders for the sentry on machine-gun emplacements.

He will be informed of any unusual circumstances noticed by his predecessor.

The relieving No. 1 will inspect the gun and ensure that the gun is in firing order, also that all necessary equipment is in place. He will be informed of any special fire orders which may have been issued for that gun.

All the foregoing is applicable to internal relief within a gun detachment. For relief of sentries when sections or companies are concerned see paras. 5 and 6.

5. *Relief of detachments.*—The guide with the relieving detachment will lead them to the dug-out of the detachment to be relieved, and report to the gun-commander of that detachment that the relieving detachment has arrived.

The relieving N.C.O. or man in charge will :—

(a) Ascertain the positions of the gun, the sentry, alternative emplacements, his officer's headquarters, the nearest telephone, and the latrine.

(b) Take over and give a receipt for trench stores.

(c) Receive a report from his No. 1 when his gun &c., is present and correct.

(d) Ensure that his No. 1 understands his orders, range card, &c., for his gun, and show him the alternative emplacements.

(e) Order his No. 1 to mount his tripod (and gun, if relief is by night), and see that this is done correctly.

(f) Detail his first sentry, and instruct him to take over.

(g) Report to his officer, " Relief complete."

(h) Draw out a duty roster.

6. The relieving sentry will ascertain the orders for the sentry as detailed in para. 4, and, in addition, will find out :—

(a) Whether the gun has been fired during the previous relief.

(b) If so, at what target, and from what emplacement.

7. The officer in charge of the relieving detachment will :—

(a) On arrival in the trench sector to be defended by his guns report to the officer of the guns to be relieved.

(b) Remain with him and receive reports from his gun commanders.

(c) Receive any instructions or information with regard to the situation, other than those he has learnt during his previous reconnaissance.

(d) As soon as the relieved detachment has moved off he will go round all his guns and make sure that his gun commanders have carried out their work correctly. At the same time he will see that any special orders he may have issued with regard to work to be done, standing fire orders, &c., are being complied with.

(e) Report "Relief complete" to his machine-gun company commander and to the company commander of the trench sector in which he finds himself.

(f) See that his arrangements for communication are on a satisfactory basis.

8. Officers in charge of detachments relieved will not move off until their detachments are reported closed up and complete.

9. *Action in trenches.*

(a) *By day.*—On the command *Action*, the sentry runs to the dug-out, wakes the other numbers, takes the gun to the emplacement, mounts, loads and lays; No. 2 follows immediately with the ammunition and first-aid case, and the remaining numbers stand by in the dug-out. When the occupants of the trench are ordered to *Stand-to*, the above procedure is carried out by the machine-gun detachments, except that the gun is only half loaded.

The loophole (if blinded) would have to be cleared before fire could be opened; the actual moment when this should be done depends on the nature of the situation.

(b) *By night.*—On the command *Action*, No. 1 will complete the loading motions. The sentry will waken the men in the dug-out and return to his post.

(c) Practice should be given in mounting the gun on the auxiliary mounting in alternative positions during drill by day to represent the Mark IV mounting having been destroyed.

Practice will also be given with the pivot and ammunition box mountings.

10. *Prepare to Advance.*

(a) *By day.*—The sentry will run to the dug-out and warn the other numbers. Nos. 1 and 2 will carry out their duties as laid down for the caution *Prepare to Advance* in " Auxiliary Mounting Drill " (Section **19** (6)). After this is completed they will carry the gun from the dug-out to the correct place in the trench. No. 3 will come up and dismount the tripod.

(b) *By night.*—Nos. 1 and 2 will be in their proper positions (see para. 3), spare parts, short length of belt and two belt boxes in the emplacement, spare numbers in the dug-out. On the command *Prepare to Advance*, No. 1 will unload, withdraw the web belt, insert the short length, perform half the loading motions, throw the short length over the feed block and release the lock spring; while No. 2 warns the spare numbers in the dug-out. The latter then returns to the gun, helps No. 1 to dismount, opens the auxiliary legs, and both adjust the leather straps. The gun is then brought to the easiest place from which to climb over the parapet, two belt boxes, spare parts, &c., being brought with it. No. 3 dismounts the tripod when the emplacement is clear, and awaits further orders.

(c) On the command *One-man Load, Action*, or *Two-man Load, Action*, either by day or night.—Nos. 1 and 2 will act as laid down in Section **19**, (7) and (8). No 3 will assist Nos. 1 and 2 with their equipment over the parapet.

(d) At this stage the instructor may either:—
  (i) Give the command *Out of Action*, on which the gun numbers will retire with the gun to their original position, or
  (ii) Order No. 3 to advance with Mark IV tripod and mount it near Nos. 1 and 2, taking care that there is no crowding of men.

22. *Section tactical exercises.*

1. Section tactical exercises will include all details of training that a section of machine-guns should receive from the section officer. If these exercises are carefully prepared and executed, the section officer on service will be relieved from the necessity of supervising the detailed execution of his orders, and will be left free to devote his attention to the general situation, while maintaining control of the movements and actions of his guns.

2. *Exercises with one gun.*—The position of readiness will be not closer to the gun position than about 50 yards. Instead of indicating the exact position on which the tripod will be set up, the instructor will mark two points about 30 yards apart, between which the gun will come into action. The ground selected should afford practice in firing in the positions described in rough ground drill (Section **20**).

Whenever possible, there should be only one small portion of the prescribed frontage from which the objective can be seen when the gun is in action. By this means the detachment will be practised in selecting suitable gun positions to meet the particular requirements of the situation, and thus develop an eye for ground.

In these exercises attention will be paid to the following points :—

- (a) The use of ground to obtain the greatest possible concealment in approaching the gun position from the position of readiness. This should be kept in mind by the instructor in selecting positions.
- (b) The method of approach to the gun position as regards carrying the gun, tripod and ammunition box. Concealment is of greater importance than rapidity within reasonable limits.
- (c) Proficiency in the lessons taught in rough ground drill. Observers will be sent out to note visibility in the approach, in mounting, and when the gun and detachment are in action.

3. *Exercises with two guns.*—The entire sub-section will be exercised with two guns on the same progressive lines as those laid down in para. 2. The actual position of each gun will be marked by the instructor in order to bring out the handling of the section with reference to the ground and the requirements of the situation. The tactical situation should be described in greater detail than is necessary for elementary drill purposes in order to employ scouts and rangetakers in a realistic manner. A simple tactical situation should be given and ranges actually taken. The position of the gun limber, of which the corporal will be in charge, will

be represented by a handcart or indicated by a flag. The supply of ammunition will be actually carried out, empty boxes being returned. The men will be changed round at intervals so that each may be exercised in the duties of the various numbers.

4. The points to be attended to in rough ground drill (Section 20) and in tactical exercises with one gun (para. 2) should be carefully observed and the performance criticised.

5. Further instruction should be given by carrying out a certain number of elementary tactical exercises, involving all duties of machine-gun section or sub-section establishments, with a view to developing co-operation between the gun numbers and initiative. These exercises should comprise movements of various kinds over a wider stretch of country than hitherto attempted. Complete exercises should be prepared in detail, with maps, instructions and points for criticism.

When possible, trained men should be used to demonstrate the methods employed.

6. Schemes should also be framed for the purpose of training machine-gun officers in the tactical principles laid down in Infantry Training and Field Service Regulations, as well as those given in this manual, and in Notes for Infantry Officers on Trench Warfare. These exercises should involve the rapid appreciation of a situation, the issue of orders to meet the situation and the control of machine-guns.

The actual presence of guns on such tactical schemes is of value, in order to test to some extent the feasibility of the execution of the orders given. Their presence, however is not essential for the conduct of the exercise.

CHAPTER V.
FIRE DIRECTION.
23. *General Remarks.*

1. The theory of rifle fire and its practical application discussed in Chapter III of the Musketry Regulations is equally applicable to the fire of machine guns, due regard being had to the greater concentration or closer grouping of shots produced by the fire of a machine gun than by the fire of an equivalent number of rifles.

2. The principal methods of machine gun fire are dealt with in Infantry Training, Sec. 162. Some further methods are given in this chapter.

3. It must be remembered that these methods are not suitable for Lewis guns, but only for machine-guns fired from a fixed platform, such as the Mark IV tripod.

4. Various tables for use in these methods of fire are given in Appendix A.

24. *Traversing Fire.*

1. The principles of traversing are taught during elementary gun drill and during the annual and general machine gun courses. (See also Infantry Training, Sec. 163 (1) (iii).)

2. This method of engaging a linear target possesses certain disadvantages. It is a slow method and requires careful training, and the regularity of the groups may possibly detract from the effect produced on the target. The former can be remedied to a great extent by seeking opportunities for oblique fire, thus reducing traversing to a minimum.

Fire effect from this very systematic form of traversing may be lost owing to the enemy anticipating where the next series of groups will fall. This can be overcome if the gunner is trained to apply series of groups at different parts of the linear target in turn.

3. An alternative method is the "Swinging Traverse," the traversing clamp being kept fairly loose, and the gun swung evenly and smoothly from side to side. This method may sometimes be found necessary against dense targets at close range, when the normal method would be too slow.

Using this method, a gun can distribute fire over approximately 30 yards of front in five seconds at close ranges.

25. *Searching fire.*

1. The principles of searching are demonstrated in Part I of the "Annual and General Course for Vickers, Maxim and Colt Guns." It is used when only one or two guns are available or combined sights will not overcome ranging errors. It requires much skill on the part of the firer to avoid gaps. The size of the groups fired will depend on the nature of the target engaged.

2. When one gun is being employed in "Searching" the sights are adjusted so that the first group will include the lowest limit of range to be searched, which is dependent on the probable error to be expected in estimating the range. The gun is then laid on the aiming mark, and the sights adjusted without relaying, so that the last group will include the highest limit of range. The line of sight will now strike the ground short of the aiming mark. (See Plate XXII.) A group will now be fired, after which the elevating whee

will be so turned as to cause the next group to strike sufficiently far beyond the first to ensure an overlap. This is continued until the line of sight is again brought on to the aiming mark.

3. When using two guns the left gun will act as described above; the sights of the right gun will be adjusted in the first instance to the highest limit, and will work down to the lowest limit. (See Plate XXIII.)

4. Searching will be discontinued if observation of results is obtained.

5. The effect of ground rising with respect to the line of sight must be considered when combined sights or searching is employed. (See Musketry Regulations, Sec. 187.)

6. Combined sights, searching, or a combination of both can also be used for engaging targets of great depth, such as roads, bridges, &c.

26. *Combined sights.*

Combined sights is a method of increasing the beaten zone by ordering two or more guns to engage the same target with different elevations. It can be used to engage targets of great depth, or it may be employed to ensure that the target shall fall within the beaten zone, when the range to the target is uncertain. (See Plate XXI.)

The table below shows the number of guns required, and the differences for 5 per cent., 10 per cent., and 15 per cent. errors in ranging. The table is not extended to include a larger number of guns than 4, as on service a section would most probably be the largest unit under the control of a single Fire Commander.

Combined Sights Table.

75 per cent. Effective Beaten Zone.				90 per cent. Effective Beaten Zone.			
Estimated Range.	Error in Ranging. Per cent	Least No. of Guns.	Differences between Guns.	Estimated Range.	Error in Ranging. Per cent	Least No. of Guns.	Differences between Guns.
700 & 800	15	2	100	1000 & 1100	15	2	100
900 & 1000	10 15	2 3	100 100	1200 & 1300	10 15	2 3	100 100
1100	10 15	3 4	100 100	1400	10 15	3 4	100 100
1200	5 10	2 4	50 50	1500	5 10	2 3	100 100
1300	5	2	50 50	1600	5 10	2 3	100 100
1400 1500 & 1600	5	3	50 50	1700 to 2000 inclusive	5 10	2 4	100 100
1700 to 2100	5	4	50	2100 & above	5	2	100

The number of variables in the table above makes it difficult to lay down any accurate rule for the employment of combined sights. For average service conditions the following will be found to give good results :

RULE.—Always use as many guns as possible : with 100 yards differences, if error in ranging is probably considerable ; 50 yards differences if error in ranging is probably small.

27. *Overhead fire.*

1. Overhead fire with machine guns may be employed under certain conditions. The following factors, all of which tend to increase the difficulty and risk, necessitate the working out of a reasonable margin of safety.

(a) The state of the barrel.
(b) The condition of the tripod and the nature of the ground on which mounted.
(c) The degree of visibility of the target.
(d) Errors due to ranging and climatic conditions.
(e) Accuracy of laying and holding by the firer.

2. The flat trajectory of modern ammunition necessarily restricts overhead fire at the closer ranges, if the gun position, friendly troops, and the enemy are approximately in the same horizontal plane; while at long ranges the dispersion of the cone of fire and difficulty in ranging make it necessary to insist on ample precautions being taken to ensure safety.

3. Overhead fire, therefore, may normally only be employed under the following conditions:—

(a) When the distance to the target has been obtained accurately; that is, by a highly-trained rangetaker, who is able to guarantee the distance within five per cent. of error.
(b) When the No. 1 at the gun is an expert firer.
(c) When an angle of not less than 30 minutes is formed by the intersection of imaginary lines drawn from the target and friendly troops to the gun, the distance to the target being 1,000 yards or under. If the distance to the target is over 1,000 yards, the angle thus formed should be not less than 60 minutes, if over 1,500 yards not less than

100 minutes, provided always that fire must cease whenever the friendly troops reach a distance of 2,000 yards from the gun, since the position of the lowest shot over this range is uncertain.

The above angles give a sufficient margin of safety at 1,000, 1,500 and 2,000 yards respectively. At distances within 1,000 yards, between 1,000 and 1,500 yards, and between 1,500 and 2,000 yards, the margin of safety continually increases. In order to obtain these safety angles, it will often be necessary to seek commanding positions for the guns, *i.e.*, rising ground, upper stories of houses, &c.

4. The foregoing instructions may be modified provided accurate and reliable observation is ensured. This, however, is a matter for the exercise of judgment and commonsense on the part of the machine-gun commander. Too much reliance must not be placed on the ability of an observer to pick up the cone of fire during an attack. The fire of the attacking troops, the supporting troops and the artillery will probably be such that the machine-gun cone of fire cannot be observed correctly.

5. The safety angles may be obtained as follows :—

(*a*) From prismatic field glasses, graticuled for Mark VII ammunition. In this case the distance between the zero line and the 600 yards graticule gives the required angle for 1,000 yards and under ; the distance between the zero line and the 1,000 yards graticule will give the angle for distances between 1,000 and 1,500 yards, and the distance between the zero line and the 1,300 yards graticule will give the angle for distances between 1,500 and 2,000 yards.

(*b*) With the aid of the graticule card as follows :—

Hold the card vertically and at the full length of the cord from the eye ; the space between the safety lines marked will then give the required angles. (See Plate XXIV.)

(c) By means of the tangent sight:—

Lay the gun on the target with the correct elevation; then move the slide up 300 yards for all ranges up to 2,000 yards without altering the elevation of the gun; and adopt the auxiliary aiming mark thus found. (See Plate XXV.)

With the tangent sight method, the firer must note carefully the auxiliary aiming mark obtained after raising the slide, and relay on this mark. If he is traversing, he must find a second auxiliary aiming mark at the other end of the line to be traversed, and must traverse along an imaginary line joining the two auxiliary aiming marks and parallel to the enemy's position.

The tangent sight method and either graticuled glasses or a graticule card should be used simultaneously, in conjunction with and as a check on each other.

When the heads of the friendly troops become visible to the firer over the sights, he should not cease fire, but should elevate his gun, taking the *enemy position* as his auxiliary aiming mark. This will cause the cone of fire to search ground in rear of the enemy's position, which may be occupied by his supports and reserves.

*28. *Indirect fire.*

1. On occasions indirect fire may be used. This form of fire is rendered possible by the Mark IV tripod of the machine gun. Guns not fired from a fixed platform must *never* be used for indirect fire.

---

* NOTE.—This section does not deal with *overhead* indirect fire or with searching reverse slopes, for which see paras. 30 and 31 respectively.

2. Indirect fire may be of great value in annoying the enemy and affecting his morale, but, except under unusually favourable conditions, cannot be expected to inflict serious loss.

The main disadvantages of indirect fire are that it requires, in most cases, a great deal of preparation and accuracy in calculation. Unless officers possess experience, it may sometimes be employed under conditions where direct fire is not only possible but necessary. Under certain conditions it may be positively dangerous to our own troops.

3. As the target is invisible, the problems to be solved are :—

How to lay the gun, both to obtain and to put on elevation and direction; and

How to maintain the laying.

The methods of solving these problems are given in skeleton form in the following table. The actual details of each of the methods are given in the subsequent paragraphs.

INDIRECT FIRE TABLE.

—	Direction.	See par.	Elevation.	See par.
Obtained by	Posts, direct	8	Graticules	4
	Map and compass	9		
	Map, protractor and reference object	10	Contoured map	5
Put on gun by	Posts and compass	11	Elevation dial	6
	Reference object and direction dial	12	Tangent sight	7
Maintained by	Auxiliary aiming mark	15	Auxiliary aiming mark	13
	Direction dial	16	Elevation dial	14

Sec. 28.] 47

4. *To obtain elevation by means of graticules.*

By means of graticules cut across the focal plane of a pair of prismatic field-glasses, or by graticules printed on a card with a string for a base, indirect fire can be as quickly applied as ordinary direct fire. These graticules are similar to an inverted backsight and represent the angles of elevation for the gun. The topmost graticule represents zero, and the lines below represent every 100 yards upwards, from 200 yards.

The procedure is as follows :—
  (i) Obtain the range to the target.
  (ii) Select an auxiliary aiming mark visible to the firer and directly above the target.
  (iii) Move to a position whence the target and the auxiliary aiming mark already chosen can be observed; look at the target in such a way that the graticule, representing the range to the target, falls across the target; then see which graticule falls across this aiming mark. (See Plate XXVI.)

The range corresponding to this graticule is the tangent elevation at which to open fire, using the aiming mark already chosen to lay on. By this means accuracy may be obtained from a gun which is invisible to the enemy. It is important to get an aiming mark vertically above the target, making any necessary allowance for wind. This method becomes inaccurate when the eye of the observer using the graticuled glasses is much below or above the gun.

If it is found necessary to increase or decrease the elevation after fire has been opened, the following method must be employed since the position of the slide does not indicate the range to the target. The range on the sights is the range for the aiming mark and not the actual range to the target, *e.g.*, the sights may show 500 yards when the target is 1,200 yards away. If in this case the cone of fire is observed to fall 100 yards short of the target, the necessary correction will not be obtained by moving the slide of the tangent sight up to 600 yards. It will be necessary to move the slide up for the same distance as from 1,200 yards to 1,300 yards. In moving the slide up for all ranges below 1,500 yards, as many clicks can be heard on the ratchet of the tangent sight as there are hundreds of yards in the range, *e.g.*, between 1,000 and 1,100 yards there are 10 clicks, between 1,100 and 1,200 yards 11 clicks, and so on. In the present example, therefore, it will be necessary to move the slide up for 12 clicks. If the cone of fire were falling 50 yards short, it would be necessary to move the slide up for 6 clicks.

This method of indirect fire must not be employed when firing over the heads of our own troops.

5. *To obtain elevation by means of a contoured map.*

Having noted on the map the exact positions of gun and target, measure the distance between them. From Table I., Appendix A, obtain the corresponding angle of tangent elevation.

From the map note the contours on which the gun and target lie and by subtraction obtain the difference in height between them. By means of the angle of sight formula,*

---

* NOTE.—The "angle of sight" can be calculated by means of the following approximate formula :—

$$\frac{VI}{HE} \times 3400 = \text{angle of sight in minutes.}$$

Where VI and HE are in the same denomination.

To convert yards to metres deduct 1/10th.

To convert metres to yards add 1/10th.

From Tables in Appendix A the quadrant angle can be obtained directly without working out the angle of sight.

knowing the range and the difference in height between gun and target, work out the angle of sight. If the angle of sight is found to be positive, add it to the angle of tangent elevation to obtain the angle of quadrant elevation necessary to put on the gun ; if, on the other hand, the angle of sight is found to be negative, subtract it.

6. *To put on elevation by means of the elevation dial.*

To place the required quadrant elevation on the gun :—
- (a) Level the gun by the spirit-level, No. 1 taking the holding pressure.
- (b) Slip the dial round till zero is under the pointer without disturbing the bubble.
- (c) Clamp the dial to, but without disturbing the elevating wheel.
- (d) Turn the elevating wheel till the required angle is obtained. One revolution of the elevating wheel produces 4° of elevation or depression on the gun. To obtain an angle of elevation of 8° the elevating wheel would have to be revolved twice. The elevation dial is accordingly graduated to 4°, showing sub-divisions of five minutes, which are easily capable of sub-division by eye.
- (e) If an obstruction exists between gun and target, make sure before firing that the shots will clear it. (See para. 17.)

7. *To put on elevation by means of the tangent sight.*

This method entails the use of an auxiliary aiming mark which must be at least 100 yards distant from the gun.

To put elevation on the gun by means of the tangent sight, convert the angle of quadrant elevation (see para. 5 above) into a range by reference to Table I., Appendix A.

Then level the gun by the spirit level, No. 1 taking the holding pressure.

Any of the four following cases may occur:—

(a) Quadrant elevation is positive and a suitable natural auxiliary aiming mark can be seen or an artificial one put out.

(b) Quadrant elevation is negative and a suitable natural auxiliary aiming mark can be seen or an artificial one put out.

(c) Quadrant elevation is positive, but there is no suitable natural auxiliary aiming mark, nor can an artificial one be placed in position.

(d) Quadrant elevation is negative, but there is no suitable natural auxiliary aiming mark, nor can an artificial one be placed in position.

Cases (c) and (d) may occur when the ground slopes down steeply in front of the gun.

Case (a).—With sights at zero, look along the sights and select a natural aiming mark or place one out and lay on it. Run the tangent sight up to the range found above and relay on the auxiliary aiming mark.

Case (b).—Run the tangent sight up to the range found above (disregarding the sign), maintaining the holding. Select a suitable natural aiming mark or place one out and lay on it. Run the sights down to zero and relay on the auxiliary aiming mark.

Case (c).—Run the tangent sight up till some suitable natural or artificial auxiliary aiming mark is visible and lay on it. Note the range on the tangent sight and convert into an angle by means of the table given in Appendix A. Add to this angle the angle of quadrant elevation found as.

[Sec. 28.]

in (para. 5). Convert the answer into a range by means of the table given in Appendix A. Run the sights up to this range and relay.

Case (d).—Run the tangent sight up till some suitable natural or artificial auxiliary aiming mark is visible and lay on it. Note the range on the tangent sight and convert into an angle by means of the table given in Appendix A. Subtract from this angle the angle of quadrant elevation found as in para. 5. Convert the answer into a range by means of the table given in Appendix A. Run the sights down to this range and relay.

8. *To obtain direction by posts, direct.*

By day, an observer selects the gun position and also the target he wishes to engage. He places a stick (L) (see Fig. 1) in the ground in rough alignment between the target and gun position. He then crawls back and, if necessary, places a second stick (L_2) in exact alignment with his first

Fig. 1.

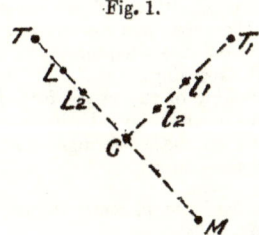

stick (L) and the target, continuing the process until his last stick is visible from the gun position (G). If it is probable that more than one target is to be engaged, other sticks (l^1, l^2) can be placed between the stick (G) and the different targets (T, T^1). To do this an assistant is required to place the sticks in position while the observer dresses them from G. It is necessary to place the sticks vertically in the ground, and the stick (G) should not be more than 6 inches above the ground to avoid being knocked over by the crosshead of the tripod when it is placed over it.

Should it be found impossible to place the stick (L) in position owing to the proximity of the enemy, the stick (G) should first be placed in position, and a second stick (M) placed in rear of it and in alignment with (G) and the target.

Under cover of darkness the position of (L) can be easily ascertained by an observer at (M) directing an assistant to place a stick in alignment with (M) and (G).

9. *To obtain direction by map and compass.*

To direct fire on to a target invisible to the guns, a map having a scale of not less than 1/20,000 must be used. The *exact* position of the guns must be marked also. This can be done by resection (see Chapter XIV, Manual of Map Reading and Field Sketching).

The magnetic bearing of the target from the gun position must be worked out on the map. If the target to be engaged is a linear one, the magnetic bearings of its limits must be worked out in the same way.

10. *To obtain direction by map, protractor and reference object.*

The exact position of the gun must be marked on the map as directed in para. 9 above. If possible, a reference object should be selected, which is marked on the map

Sec. 28.] 53

and visible from the gun position. If the only suitable reference object visible from the gun position is *not* marked on the map, its magnetic bearing should be taken from the gun position, and a line showing its direction drawn through the gun position on the map.

On the map by means of a protractor measure the angle included between lines joining the target and the gun, and the reference object and the gun. (See Fig. 2.) If the target to be engaged is a linear one, measure the angles included between lines joining its limits to the gun and the target to the gun.

Fig. 2.

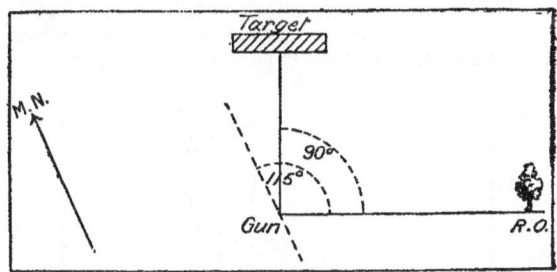

11. *To lay for direction by means of a post and compass.*

To lay out an aiming post, drive in a stick (not more than 6 inches high) at the gun position, and place a compass on top. Rotate the compass till the dial indicates the required magnetic bearing found as directed in para. 9. Dress a post on this bearing, using the hair line on the compass glass.

Replace the gun and tripod on the first stick and lay on the post put out.

12. *To lay for direction by means of reference object and direction dial.*

The gun is laid on any convenient part of the reference object with the sights set for any convenient range; it need not be levelled. The elevation required to hit the target should not be placed on the gun till the latter is directed on the target. The direction dial should now be set to read zero (or the reading noted if the dial cannot be rotated). The gun is then swung right or left through the angle found as directed in para. 10, according as the reference object is to the left or right of the target. The gun can be directed to either end of a linear target simply by swinging through the angles found as directed in para. 10. (See Fig. 3.)

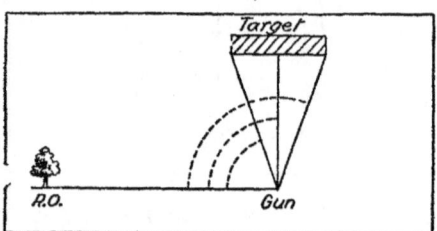

13. *To maintain elevation by means of an auxiliary aiming mark and the tangent sight.*

Once the gun has been laid the sights only may be adjusted so as to bring a line of sight on to any suitable natural or artificial auxiliary aiming mark, e.g., a night firing-box, white or luminous stone, chimney, post, &c. The range shown on the tangent sight after such adjustment will have no connection with the quadrant elevation on the gun, unless the elevation has been put on by the method given in para. 7, and the same auxiliary aiming mark is used to maintain it.

The distance between the gun and the auxiliary aiming mark is immaterial when *maintaining* elevation, and in this respect differs from the minimum distance laid down in para. 7 when *putting on* elevation.

14. *To maintain elevation by the elevation dial.*

Between bursts of fire the firer should make sure that the pointer continues to show the same quadrant elevation on the dial as was originally put on the gun. If this method is to be reliable it is essential that the legs of the tripod should not sink unevenly into the ground ; the tripod must, therefore, be placed on a firm foundation.

It is desirable, where possible, to use an auxiliary aiming mark in addition, but if this is not possible the spirit level should be placed on the gun at frequent intervals, and the procedure laid down in para. 6 for putting on elevation repeated. It should be noted that unless the socket is absolutely upright, the quadrant elevation may vary considerably if the gun is traversed through a wide arc, though the reading of the elevation dial will not alter.

15. *To maintain direction by means of an auxiliary aiming mark.*

See para. 13 above.

16. *To maintain direction by means of the direction dial.*

The gun having been laid for direction, the reading of the direction dial is noted. Direction can be maintained during firing by ensuring that the pointer is set accurately to this reading.

17. In all cases where the target is invisible owing to the presence of an obstacle, steps must be taken before firing to ensure that the shots will clear the obstacle. The procedure is as follows :—

- (a) After the gun has been given the quadrant elevation necessary to hit the target, the tangent sight will be adjusted for the range to the top of the obstacle. If on looking along the sights the obstacle is not visible, the shots will clear. If, however, the obstacle *is* visible, the shots will not clear, and the gun must be moved further back.
- (b) If the range to the obstacle is under 100 yards, the method given above will not apply, and the No. 1 must look through the barrel, either directly or by using the mirror reflector.
- (c) Should the obstacle be invisible from the gun position recourse must be had to the formula given in Section **30**, para. 4 (*l*). The clearance required will be one half of the height of the 90 per cent. cone at the range of the obstacle. In using the formula given in Section **30**, para. 4 (*l*), for " our own troops " read " the obstacle " throughout.

29. *Night firing.*

1. If the gun position is not exposed to the enemy's fire or to direct observation, the gun can be mounted and laid by day and left until night.

Sec. 29.]

Some kind of auxiliary aiming mark must be in position in front of the gun for the purpose of maintaining elevation and direction after nightfall. (See Section 28.)

This auxiliary aiming mark can be a transparent screen secured to the open side of a box containing some form of illuminant. (See Fig. 1.) The screen is marked with lines to permit of searching and traversing within definite limits. The horizontal lines are 1 inch apart, which will give a difference in angle of 10 minutes from the centre line if the screen is placed 10 yards from the gun. The amount that 10 minutes represents in range can be readily ascertained from the tables showing the angles of elevation for the gun (Appendix A, Table 1). The vertical lines are 2½ inches apart, which will give a deflection of about 2 feet per 100 yards of range when the screen is placed 10 yards from the gun.

Fig. 1.

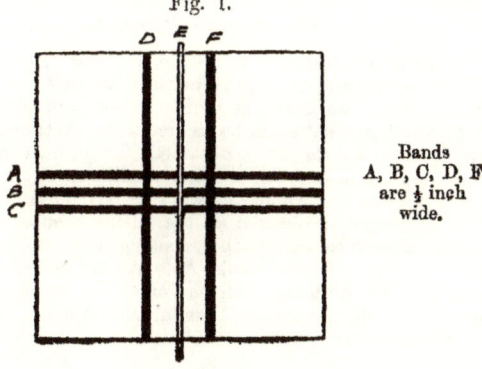

Bands A, B, C, D, F are ½ inch wide.

2. When the gun position is exposed, or the gun is required elsewhere during the day, it will sometimes be possible for arrangements to be made by day so that the gun and tripod can be brought up under cover of darkness and placed in position to open fire when required. (See Section 23.)

The direction and elevation dials should be employed; and a luminous reference object should be laid out in any convenient position, where it is invisible to the enemy, for obtaining the direction to any target, correct elevation being put on by the elevation dial.

As the rear leg of the tripod may sink during firing, elevation cannot be maintained by means of the elevation dial, which is a component part of the mounting. One or more luminous auxiliary aiming marks should therefore be laid out by the method given in Section 28, para. 8.

20. *Indirect overhead fire.*

1. In trench warfare, where the positions of our own and the enemy's units are clearly marked, indirect fire over the heads of our own troops may often be safely employed.

2. The best results will be secured when observation of the strike of the bullets can be obtained. The element of chance, due to errors in ranging, climatic conditions, errors as to the exact position of the gun, &c., will thus be removed.

3. Fire may be directed on the hostile support or reserve lines, communication trenches, cooking places, ration parties, reverse slopes of hills, roads, &c. When observation is not possible, the most that can be done is to sweep an area of ground, in which is included the target it is desired to engage. (See Section 31.)

4. To ensure the safety of our own troops the following rules must at all times be strictly adhered to:—

(a) The guns must never be more than 2,000 yards distant from bodies of our own troops, over whom they are firing.

(b) When the guns are 1,000 yards or under from our own troops, the range at which they are fired must be such as to ensure the centre of the cone of fire passing at least 20 yards over their heads. (See Trajectory Table, Appendix A.)

When the guns are between 1,000 yards and 1,500 yards from our own troops this height must be at least 40 yards; between 1,500 and 2,000 yards it must be at least 80 yards.

(c) When the gun, friendly troops, and target are all on the same plane (not necessarily the same *horizontal* plane), rules (a) and (b) give the following results:—

(i) No target may be engaged at a range of less than 1,500 yards.

(ii)
Range to target in yards.	Limits of safety zone for friendly troops, in yards.
1,500	700 to 1,000 from gun.
1,600	500 „ 1,000 „ „
1,700	500 „ 1,000 „ „
1,800	400 „ 1,200 „ „
1,900	400 „ 1,500 „ „
2,000	300 „ 1,500 „ „
2,100	300 „ 1,500 „ „
2,200	300 „ 1,500 „ „
2,300	200 „ 1,800 „ „
2,400 and over	200 „ 2,000 „ „

(d) Climatic conditions must be carefully studied (See Musketry Regulations, Sec. 29.)
(e) The laying must be checked frequently, both for direction and elevation, upon the auxiliary aiming mark.
(f) The necessity for good holding must be impressed on the firer.
(g) As a slight sinking of the tripod during firing may seriously affect the safety of our own troops, owing to the altered angle of elevation, every precaution must be taken to prevent this happening. The legs of the tripod should be firmly embedded in the ground, and provision made to prevent them moving from their original position, but the use of an auxiliary aiming mark largely minimises the effect of slight movements of the tripod.
(h) When " traversing " or " searching " is used, provision must be made by means of wooden battens, &c., to fix safe limits beyond which the gun cannot be moved.
(i) A worn barrel should not be used, and the barrel should be cleaned after every 1,000 rounds continuous fire.
(j) All calculations must be carefully checked by an officer before fire is opened.
(k) Troops over whom fire is to be opened must be cautioned, and a certificate to this effect signed by the machine gun company commander.
(l) In order to find the clearance, *i.e.*, the height from the ground to the centre of the cone at any point in the line of fire, the following is the simplest and most accurate method, which should be used.

Sec. 30.]   61

(i) Let gun contour ... ... = A yards.
„ own troops contour ... = B „
„ centre of cone above or below horizontal plane through gun position when passing over own troops heads ... ... = C „

Then clearance (yards) = A − B $\overset{+}{_-}$ C.

C must be added or subtracted according as the trajectory to our own troops position is above or below the horizontal plane through the gun position.

(ii) From the sketch the clearance is XZ.

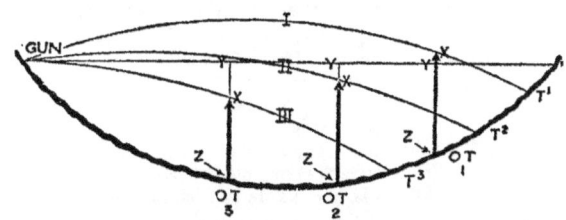

Then A − B = ZY and XY is the height of trajectory either above or below the horizontal plane through the gun position.

Obviously clearance = XZ = ZY $\overset{+}{_-}$ XY = A − B $\overset{+}{_-}$ C.

(iii) In order to find C, either Table 2A or Table 2B must be used according as to whether the quadrant angle on the gun is positive or negative. On these tables, the words "positive" and "negative" are printed. If the trajectory height found is positive, C must be added to A−B; if negative, it must be subtracted from A−B.

(iv) If the quadrant angle on the gun is positive, the range corresponding must be found from Table 1 in order to use Table 2(A). If the quadrant angle is negative it will be used directly in Table 2(B) without conversion.

(v) The following three examples illustrate the method and deal with three typical cases. (See sketch above.)

CASE I.—Quadrant angle is positive and sufficiently large to throw the centre of cone above the horizontal plane when passing over own troops heads.

EXAMPLE. Gun contour (A) = 70 yards.
Own troops contour (B) = 20 yards.
Q.E. = + 86 minutes. Range corresponding = 1,200 yards.
Assumed range to own troops 900 yards.
From Table 2(A) trajectory height for 1,200 yards at 900 yads = 9 yards (positive) = C.
Clearance = A − B + C.
= 70 − 20 + 9 = 59 yards.
Clearance required = 20 yards. It is safe to fire.

CASE II.—Quadrant angle is positive but small, so that the centre of cone is below the horizontal plane when passing over own troops heads.

EXAMPLE. A and B as above.
Q.E. = + 35 minutes. Range corresponding = 700 yards.
Assumed range to own troops 900 yards.

From Table 2(A) trajectory height for 700 yards at 900 yards = 4·5 yards (negative) = C.
Clearance = A − B − C.
= 70 − 20 − 5 (say) = 45 yards.
Clearance required = 20 yards. It is safe to fire.

CASE III.—Quadrant angle is negative.

EXAMPLE. A and B as above.
Q.E. = − 75 minutes.
Assumed range to own troops 900 yards.
From Table 2B trajectory height for −75 minutes at 900 yards = 33·2 yards (negative) = C.
Clearance = A − B − C.
= 70 − 20 − 33 (say) = 17 yards.
Clearance required = 20 yards. It is not safe to fire.

(vi) In Appendix B is given a copy of the "INDIRECT OVERHEAD FIRE" sheet which should be used on service. Certain specimen examples have been filled in on it, for the purpose of bringing out various points.

5. Elevation and direction may be obtained, put on the gun, and maintained by any of the methods described in Section **28**. The dials are particularly suitable for this type of fire.

31. *Searching reverse slopes.*

1. It may sometimes be desired to search the reverse slope of a hill occupied by the enemy, where he is under shelter from short range fire.

2. Reverse slopes are often chosen by the enemy as suitable areas where troops may be disposed preparatory to attack, or may manœuvre free from observation. It is therefore

necessary to know how such ground may be brought, most effectively, under machine gun fire. Table 7 enables the machine gun officer to search the reverse slope of a hill, and is constructed on the following basis :—

3. If a gun is placed at such a distance from the crest that the cone, just passing over it, will fall at a steeper angle than the slope of the ground on the other side of the hill, then fire effect will be brought to bear on the reverse slope. No endeavour has been made to fit the trajectory exactly to the reverse slope, as the difficulties and variables in the problem are so many, that small errors would upset the results. Traversing and searching should be employed, for the same reasons as govern all forms of indirect fire.

4. *Table 7*.—This table is so constructed, that when the gun is placed as required by its use, and fire suitably directed at the reverse slope, the bullets will fall on it at an angle of somewhere between 100 and 200 minutes to the slope itself.

The table is divided into two parts :—" Gun above crest " and " Gun below crest."

The table is used as follows :—

(a) On the map, draw a line from the crest, which will be the probable line of fire.

(b) From the map, determine the drop IN YARDS in 100 yards, measured from the crest down the slope.

(c) Making use of the two top horizontal columns, note the distance to measure back, which will vary according as the spot thus found is above or below the crest. (See centre column.)

(d) From map note the difference in height between this spot and the crest, above or below as the case may be. Run down the centre column till this height is found.

(e) Then look along horizontally, when the final range from the crest will be found in the vertical column under the drop in yards found in (b).

(f) Place the gun at this point, and lay on the crest by any suitable means.

NOTE.—If it is found that the gun position is on the same level as the crest two answers will be given, i.e., one in portion of " Gun above crest," one in portion " Gun below crest," both opposite the zero mark. Select the most suitable.

CHAPTER VI.
MACHINE-GUNS IN BATTLE.
32. *Introductory.*

1. The general principles laid down in Infantry Training, Chapter XV, for the employment of machine-guns in battle remain unaltered by the introduction of the machine-gun company organization and the substitution of Lewis gun detachments for machine-gun sections in battalions. But the new organization and the increase in the number of machine-guns with infantry units have rendered necessary certain modifications in detail which are discussed in the present chapter. A certain amount of repetition and re-arrangement of matter that is already dealt with in Infantry Training has been found necessary in order to avoid too frequent reference to paragraphs or sentences in that manual.

2. The special characteristics of Lewis guns and the manner in which these characteristics affect their employment must

be studied by machine-gun officers, as they have to co-operate closely with Lewis guns. These characteristics, therefore, are discussed in Sections **33** and **34**.* Detailed instructions for Lewis guns are given in Lewis Gun Training.†

3. The special principles which govern the employment of machine-guns in the phase of operations known as trench warfare are dealt with in " Notes for Infantry Officers on Trench Warfare."

4. It must be remembered that in Infantry Training a machine-gun section means two guns whereas under the present organisation it means two sub-sections each of two guns, or four in all.

33. *Characteristics of Machine-guns and Lewis guns compared.*

1. The principal characteristic of the machine-gun is its ability to produce *rapid and sustained fire.* Provided water and ammunition are available, a machine-gun is capable of keeping up a rapid fire for a very considerable period.

On the other hand the Lewis gun, though capable of extremely rapid fire, is incapable of sustaining this fire for long. This necessitates, therefore, the use of short bursts of fire as the normal practice.

Its inability to sustain fire is primarily due to the fact that a water jacket is not provided (in order to economise weight) and the gun consequently becomes hot very quickly. Further, owing to their lightness, the working parts will not stand constant vibration to the same extent as those of the machine gun.

---

* Infantry battalions are provided with Lewis guns organised in Lewis gun detachments of 1 N.C.O. and 12 men each, with 2 Lewis guns.
† To be issued shortly.

2. A further difference between the two weapons is in the type of mounting used. The machine-gun is provided with a heavy tripod, which enables the gun to be used for overhead and indirect fire. This mounting also allows of the gun being laid on a fixed point, and fired at any time, by day or night, without further preparation. By this means it is possible to form " bands of fire " through which any enemy attempting to pass must suffer heavy loss.

The Lewis gun is fired from the shoulder, a light bipod providing a support for the barrel; there is no traversing or elevating gear; and aim is taken and altered as when using a rifle. The conditions are, therefore, not suitable for overhead or indirect fire, nor for creating " bands of fire."

3. The machine-gun, owing to its weight, and that of its mounting, is less mobile than the Lewis gun. The latter, being specially provided with a light bipod to increase its mobility, can be carried like a rifle, and fired with very little preliminary preparation, so that after movement its fire can be brought to bear on any object much more rapidly than that of a machine-gun.

34. *The employment of Lewis guns.*

1. Owing to its greater mobility a much greater liberty of action can be allowed to this weapon than to the machine-gun. It must, however, be clearly understood that the Lewis gun cannot take the place of the machine gun. It is a supplement to, and not a substitute for, the latter type of weapon.

2. It is adapted for even closer co-operation with infantry than the machine-gun, as the Lewis gunner can move and appear to the enemy as an ordinary rifleman. Its distribution

as a battalion and company weapon provides a mobile reserve of fire available for the smallest unit commander wherever an infantry soldier can go.

3. It is specially adapted for a concentrated enfilade fire on a definite line such as a hedge or wall, or to cover a road or defile where it is not possible to deploy a number of rifles, and for places where it is difficult or impossible to bring up a machine-gun unobserved. When wider fronts have to be swept with fire or heavier fire is required at longer ranges machine guns can be more usefully employed.

4. Although the expenditure of ammunition is not so great as with machine guns, the difficulty of getting ammunition up to the more exposed positions to which Lewis guns can go will be much greater. It is important, therefore, to withhold fire as long as possible and to use the power of the gun to develop unexpected bursts of fire against favourable targets.

35. *The tactical handling of infantry machine-guns.*

1. The tactical principles laid down in Infantry Training, Sections 160, 161 and 162, apply generally, but the organization and distribution of the machine guns with a brigade there discussed need modification to suit the new organization and distribution of machine-guns.

2. The introduction of the machine-gun company organization, while facilitating the collective employment of machine-guns, does not mean that they should always be so employed. It may sometimes be advisable to detach machine-guns under the orders of battalion commanders and this should be done if the tactical situation requires it.—See section 36 (2) and

(3).—In this case the battalion commander concerned should clearly understand the reasons why the guns are attached to him. Definite instructions should be given by the battalion commander to the machine-gun officer as to what is required of him, but the latter should be allowed as much freedom as possible in the execution of his task.

3. *Command and Control.*—The various tasks, which the machine-gun company has to carry out, demand the most careful preparation and organization on the part of the company commander.

He must ensure that all section commanders fully understand the part they have to play, and he must be always on the watch to regain control, at the earliest possible moment, of any guns temporarily detached, in order to provide a reserve for his brigade commander.

During action the machine-gun company commander will keep in the closest possible touch with the brigade commander, and it is important that section officers should keep in close touch with the commanders of units to which they may be attached, and under whose command they come. Machine-gun officers must carefully observe this principle in order to avoid dual control and consequent misunderstanding.

It is unsafe to rely on telephones, especially in open fighting. Steps must, therefore, be taken to maintain communication by visual signalling and by orderlies.

4. *Co-operation.*—Co-operation is an essential feature in machine-gun tactics, both between the machine-guns and other arms and between the guns themselves.

Grouping machine-guns into companies, by centralizing control, facilitates the execution of a comprehensive scheme of machine-gun co-operation in accordance with the needs of the tactical situation. When this is to be effected the machine-gun company commander must be thoroughly conversant with the situation. He should take every step to ensure co-operation, not only between the guns of his company, but between his company and machine guns on the flanks.

5. *Concealment.*

(a) *During movement.*—To ensure concealment when on the move, machine-gunners should try to disguise their identity as such by adopting the formation of the neighbouring troops. This, and any other means of escaping detection, should be constantly practised.

When machine-guns are moving, they should watch and avoid areas that are being swept by shell fire.

(b) *When in position :—*
- (i) As few men as possible should be near the gun. It will usually be found that two men are quite sufficient.
- (ii) When time, implements, &c., are available, guns should be dug in, but, unless it is possible to construct a really satisfactory emplacement, it is better to seek cover from view. A hastily made emplacement will merely serve to draw the attention of the enemy.
- (iii) Masks and gloves will often facilitate concealment, especially when facing strong sunlight.

Every effort must be made to prevent machine-guns being located by artillery. If, however, machine-guns are shelled, their action will largely depend on the tactical situation. They may make a change in position of about 50 yards or they may temporarily cease fire, the guns and detachment getting under cover; the latter will often deceive the enemy into thinking that they have been destroyed and enable the guns to obtain a good target later. A careful distribution of the gun numbers will minimise casualties.

36. *Machine-guns in the attack.*

1. In order to obtain the best results, the machine-gun company commander must be thoroughly acquainted with the plan of operations and must make a careful reconnaissance of the ground.

By use of maps and study of the ground through a telescope from positions in rear or on the flanks, he should endeavour to make himself familiar with the nature of the ground, the correct use of which may prove of decisive value. See Infantry Training, Section 161.

Having made his reconnaissance, and having received instructions from the brigade commander (Infantry Training, Section 160 (13)), the machine-gun company commander will give definite orders to his section officers.

2. *Distribution of machine-guns in the attack.*—The machine gun company commander may divide the guns under his command into groups, some to go forward with the infantry, some to cover their advance, others as a reserve.

3. The machine-guns that go forward with the attacking infantry will be placed under the control of the infantry commander to whom they are attached. See Infantry Training, Section 160 (13).

The rôle of these guns will be to:—

    (*a*) Assist the infantry in obtaining superiority of fire.

(b) Make good the positions won.
(c) Pursue the enemy with fire.
(d) Cover re-organization of the infantry.
(e) Repel counter-attack.
(f) Cover retirement in the event of the attack proving unsuccessful.

The number of guns to be sent with the infantry will be governed by two factors, viz., the length of front and the nature of the ground. The *time* of their advance will be determined by the nature of the ground and progress of the infantry. The progress of the infantry must be carefully watched so that the guns may be brought forward at the earliest possible moment. They should very rarely advance with the leading line of infantry. This is the duty of the Lewis guns, the fire of which should suffice to hold the position won, until it can finally be consolidated by the machine-guns.

4. The guns detailed to cover the advance of the infantry will normally be under the control of the machine-gun company commander, who acts under the instructions of the brigade commander. The rôle of these guns will be to provide covering fire for the infantry up to the last possible moment in the following ways :—

(a) By fire from the flanks, or through gaps in the line.
(b) By overhead fire.
(c) By indirect fire.

Great care must be exercised in (b) and (c) in order to avoid endangering our own troops.

Orders to the machine guns detailed for this task may, if necessary, include general instructions to govern their action, after the task has been completed, pending receipt of further orders from the machine-gun company commander. It must, however, be remembered that it is usually dangerous to prescribe to a subordinate at a distance anything that he should be better able to decide on the spot, with a fuller knowledge of local conditions, for any attempt to do so may cramp his initiative in dealing with unforeseen developments. (See F.R.S., Part I., Section 12, para. 2.)

5. Guns kept as a reserve will be under the control of the machine-gun company commander, acting under the instructions of the brigade commander. Owing to their characteristics, machine-guns are valuable as a reserve of fire power, and when kept in reserve in the hands of the brigade commander may prove of the utmost value at the critical moment. It must be remembered, however, that a great development of fire power is most useful in the opening stages of an attack, to cover the advance of the infantry, and it is a mistake to keep guns in reserve if they can be usefully employed in supporting the advance. These guns may be used for long range searching fire on ground behind the enemy's line, which is likely to hold supports or reserves, but must be available to move forward at once, when required.

6. The great fire power of machine-guns relative to the space they occupy, the rapidity with which they may be brought into or out of action and the ease with which they can change the direction of their fire render them especially suitable for the protection of threatened flanks and for filling gaps which may appear laterally or in depth. Any of the guns mentioned in the previous paragraphs may at times be employed in this manner.

7. During an attack it may be advisable to continue to hold certain tactical points, which have been captured, until the

attacking troops have made good their next objective. The characteristics of machine-guns fit them for this duty; their use will avoid diminishing the strength and dash of the attacking infantry.

8. *Limbers and ammunition reserve.*—Gun limbers will generally remain under the orders of section or sub-section officers, but ammunition limbers would, as a rule, be placed under the officer in charge of the brigade ammunition reserve (Infantry Training, Section 166 (2)), or under a machine-gun officer, who should keep thoroughly in touch with the progress of the machine-guns so that he may be able to keep the wagons as close up as possible.

When machine-guns are attached to battalions, a proportion of ammunition limbers will accompany them if required.

It must be remembered that ammunition limbers are far less mobile than gun limbers.

37. *Machine-guns in the defence.*

1 When it has been decided to consolidate a position for defence a reconnaissance should be carried out, the machine-guns being generally allotted on the following principles.

2. Some guns should be posted as soon as possible in accordance with the nature of the ground to form a complete belt of flanking machine-gun fire along the front of the position. Important concealed approaches and folds in the ground should also be covered by machine guns.

Co-operation must be arranged with the Lewis guns of battalions, which can cover the less important approaches or small depressions or hollows which the machine-guns cannot sweep.

3. A proportion of machine-guns should be kept in reserve. When the ground is suitable, these may be used for indirect overhead fire if the results are likely to justify the expenditure of ammunition, and the readiness of the guns to take up other tasks is not impaired. It will often be found advisable to prepare machine-gun emplacements at important tactical points in rear of the front line and to detail guns for their occupation, if necessary. Preparation in this respect will facilitate a rapid readjustment of the line at any point.

4. Secondary positions and lines of retirement must be reconnoitred, and steps must be taken to ensure that the detachments are familiar with them. In case of a withdrawal becoming necessary, machine-guns in supporting positions will cover the retirement of the infantry and guns in the front line. When the latter have occupied their secondary positions, they, in their turn, will cover the movement of the guns originally in support.

5. Arrangements for firing at night should be made. The day and night gun positions will probably be different; the change from the one to the other should be made just after dark and just before dawn.

6. Communication must carefully be arranged throughout machine-gun sections. Machine-gun officers must keep in touch with battalion commanders and the machine-gun company commander. (See Section 35, para. 3.)

7. The following points should also be noted :—

(a) The position of the ammunition limber should be determined and the arrangements for ammunition supply made known to all concerned.

(b) Range cards should be made for each gun

8. The variations that arise during the protracted defence of a position are dealt with in "Notes for Infantry Officers on Trench Warfare."

38. *Machine-guns with an advanced guard.*

1. The functions of an advanced guard make it necessary that great fire power should be available when required. A large proportion of machine-guns should therefore be allotted to advanced guards.

These machine-guns should move well forward in the column, so that they may be able to get quickly into action.

2. The principal duties of machine-guns with the advanced guard are to:—
   - (a) Assist in driving back enemy forces by rapid production of great fire power at any required point;
   - (b) Assist in holding any position gained until the arrival of the infantry;
   - (c) Cover the deployment of the main body by holding the enemy on a wide front.

3. The characteristics of machine-guns render them as a rule more suitable for employment with the main guard than with the vanguard, but the size of the vanguard may necessitate machine-guns being attached to it.

39. *Machine-guns with a rear guard.*

1. As rear guards will usually be required to hold positions with the minimum of men, a large proportion of machine-guns should be allotted to them.

2. Experience has shown that well placed machine guns, supported by a few infantry only, will frequently hold up an advance for long periods.

3. In occupying a rear guard position with machine-guns, the ordinary principles of defence apply, but the following points should be specially noted:—

(a) As wide a field of fire as possible should be selected.
(b) Guns must be concealed in the least obvious places.
(c) Covered lines of retirement must be reconnoitred.
(d) Gun limbers should be close up to facilitate a hasty retirement.
(e) Positions in rear must be chosen before the machine-guns retire from their forward positions.
(f) A proportion of the machine-guns should occupy the positions in rear, before all the machine-guns retire from the forward position. Thus the retirement of the last gun can be covered.
(g) Pack transport is very useful.

40. *Village fighting.*

1. As soon as the infantry have made good one edge of a village, machine-guns should be brought up in close support. They should then search windows, doorways, roofs, &c., likely to be held by the enemy.

2. Machine-guns should be used to command cross-streets, &c., so as to guard against attack on the flanks or rear of the infantry. They should also be posted on the edges of the villages to prevent flank attacks, and when possible should be pushed forward well on the flanks, so as to command the exits from the village.

3. During village fighting use may be made of windows, doors, &c., as machine-gun positions. If a good field of fire cannot be obtained from existing doors and windows, and

time is available, small holes can be made in the outside walls of the upper storeys of buildings, enabling a good field of fire to be obtained.

41. *Occupation of various positions.*

1. Machine-guns may be hidden in almost any position, but it is advisable to avoid places which are either obvious or easy to recognise, such as cross-roads or single objects, or places which can easily be located on the map. It is important that guns should merge into the surroundings, and straight edges or distinct shadows should not be made.

2. Banks of rivers, canals and railways, ditches, folds in the ground, hedges, palings or walls, also mounds of earth, may be used either to afford a covered line of approach and supply to a gun position or else a gun position itself. When firing over the top of the cover, greater protection is given if hollows are scooped out for the front tripod legs. (Plates XII to XIV.)

3. Houses may be employed in the following ways:—

The gun may be placed in rear, firing through windows or doors in line or past the sides of the house. When firing from a window, door or hole in the roof, the gun should be placed well back for concealment. (Plate XVI.) A damp piece of cloth hung in front of the gun helps to conceal the flash. When firing from a cellar, care should be taken not to cause a cloud of dust to rise and give away the position. A means of retirement and alternative emplacements should be arranged. Overhead fire and observation may often be obtained from high buildings.

4. Woods and crops provide cover from view, facilities for communication, and good lines of approach or supply. In

neither case should guns be placed too near to the front edge. In woods it will often be possible to construct hasty overhead cover.

5. If a barricade has been constructed across a road, machine-guns should not be put on the barricade itself but, if possible, in a concealed position to a flank from which they can sweep the road.

6. Haystacks do not as a rule afford a very satisfactory position, but guns may be placed in a hollow in front, or behind, firing past the side, or else in a hollow on top, firing through the front face of the stack. A machine-gun concealed in a field which is covered with cornstalks, manure heaps, or mounds of roots is very hard to locate. (Plate XV.)

7. Wood stacks, planks, logs of trees, and farm implements may be used to conceal guns; cover from fire can often be obtained by the addition of bricks or sand bags. (Plate XV.)

8. Trees generally provide better observation posts than machine-gun positions.

42. Signals.

In many cases observation will be impossible from the gun position, and it will be necessary for observers to signal results from a flank. The following semaphore code is used in signalling the results of observation of fire:—

O ... = Fire observed *over*.
S ... = Fire observed *short*.
R ... = Fire observed to *right* of target.
L ... = Fire observed to *left* of target.
K ... = Fire observed *correct* (target or range).
W ... = Fire unobserved or "Wash-out."

APPENDIX A. TABLE I.—TANGENT ELEVATION, ANGLES OF DESCENT, DIMENSIONS OF CONES AND ZONES, &c. ·303 VICKERS GUN, MARK VII AMMUNITION.

1	2	3		4	5				6	
Range, Yards.	Angle of Tangent Elevation. Minutes.	Slope of Descent.		Height in yards of lowest shot below cr. of cone.	Dimensions in yards of horizontal beaten zones.				Dimensions of cones in yards.	
		In Minutes.	As a Gradient.		Width.		Length.		Width.	Height.
					75 p.c.	90 p.c.	75 p.c.	90 p.c.	75 p.c.	75 p.c.
100	3	—	—	—	—	—	—	—	—	—
200	7	—	—	—	—	—	—	—	—	—
300	11	—	—	1.0	—	—	—	—	—	—
400	16	15	One in 230	1.3	.3	.3	—	—	.3	1.5
500	22	23	,, 149	1.7	.5	.5	—	—	.5	1.9
600	28	32	,, 107	2.0	.7	.7	—	—	.7	2.3
700	35	42	,, 82	2.3	.8	2.3	220	700	.8	2.7
800	43	54	,, 64	2.7	1.0	2.8	204	600	1.0	3.1
900	52	69	,, 50	3.0	1.2	3.3	188	525	1.2	3.6
1000	62	88	,, 39	3.3	1.3	3.8	172	450	1.3	4.1
1100	73	111	,, 31	3.7	1.5	4.3	156	375	1.5	4.1
1200	86	139	,, 25	4.0	1.7	5.0	140	300	1.7	4.5
1300	101	172	,, 20	4.7	2.0	6.0	126	270	2.0	4.9
1400	117	209	,, 16	5.3	2.3	7.0	112	240	2.3	5.2
1500	135	251	,, 14	6.0	2.7	8.0	98	210	2.7	5.4
1600	155	298	,, 12	6.7	3.0	9.0	84	180	3.0	5.8
1700	177	350	,, 9.8	7.3	3.3	10.0	75	160	3.3	6.3
1800	201	407	,, 8.5	8.0	3.7	11.3	70	150	3.7	6.8
1900	227	469	,, 7.3	8.7	4.0	12.7	70	145	4.0	7.7
2000	256	541	,, 6.4	9.3	4.7	14.0	70	140	4.7	8.3
2100	288	623	,, 5.5	10.0	5.3	15.3	70	135	5.3	9.0
2200	322	715	,, 4.8	13.3	6.7	16.7	74	140	6.7	9.9
2300	360	817	,, 4.2	16.7	8.0	18.0	78	150	8.0	10.9
2400	401	929	,, 3.7	20.0	9.3	19.3	82	160	9.3	13.4
2500	447	1052	,, 3.3	25.0	10.7	20.7	86	170	10.7	16.2
2600	496	1186	,, 2.9	30.0	12.0	22.0	90	180	12.0	19.5
2700	551	1332	,, 2.6	35.0	13.3	23.3	100	190	13.3	23.2
2800	610	1491	,, 2.3	41.7	16.7	25.0	110	200	16.7	27.2
2900				48.3	20.0	26.7			20.0	34.5
3000					23.3	28.3	120	210	23.3	42.3
										52.1

APPENDIX A. TABLE 2 (A).— TRAJECTORY TABLE.

·303 VICKERS GUN, MARK VII AMMUNITION.

Range. Yards.	Point Distant from Gun in Yards.																												
	200	300	400	500	600	700	800	900	1000	1100	1200	1300	1400	1500	1600	1700	1800	1900	2000	2100	2200	2300	2400	2500	2600	2700	2800	
0	·4																											
100	·2	·7	1.0	1.9	3.2	4.9	7.1	10.0	13.6	18.0	23.4	30.2	38.2	47.6	58.9	72.2	87.5	105	125	149								
200	0	·5	1.5	2.8	4.5	6.5	9.4	12.8	17.2	22.4	29.0	37.3	46.4	57.0	70.7	86.0	104	124	147									
300	·3	·3	1.1	2.3	3.7	5.7	8.4	11.8	16.0	21.0	27.6	35.5	44.8	55.0	68.3	84.0	102	121	145									
400	·5	0	·6	1.6	3.0	4.9	7.5	10.8	14.8	19.3	25.7	33.4	43.1	54.2	66.7	82.6	100	119	142									
500	·9	·3	·9	·9	2.1	3.9	6.3	9.5	13.3	18.3	24.5	32.6	41.7	52.8	65.7	81.3	99	117	140									
600	1.2	1.4	1.3	·6	0	1.4	3.5	6.3	9.8	14.4	20.2	27.6	36.1	46.6	59.0	73.6	90.6	110	133									
700	1.6	2.0	2.1	1.7	·9	0	1.9	4.5	7.9	12.3	17.8	25.0	33.3	43.6	55.5	70.1	87.0	106	128									
800	2.1	2.7	3.1	3.1	2.6	1.6	0	2.4	5.5	9.9	15.2	21.9	30.0	40.1	52.0	66.1	82.7	102	124									
900	2.6	3.5	4.1	4.4	4.2	3.5	2.0	0	2.9	6.7	11.9	18.5	26.4	36.2	48.3	61.7	78.0	96.6	119									
1000	3.3	4.3	5.3	5.9	5.9	5.5	4.4	2.6	0	3.5	8.7	14.7	22.4	31.8	43.2	56.9	72.8	91.1	113									
1100	3.9	5.4	6.8	7.5	7.8	7.8	7.1	5.6	3.3	0	4.5	10.6	17.9	27.0	38.1	51.4	67.0	85.0	106									
1200	4.6	6.5	8.1	9.3	10.2	10.3	10.1	9.0	7.1	4.2	0	5.7	12.6	21.4	32.1	45.0	60.1	78.0	98.9									
1300	5.5	7.8	9.5	11.3	12.5	13.7	13.2	12.8	11.6	9.1	5.1	0	6.0	14.8	25.1	37.5	52.3	69.5	90.5									
1400	6.4	9.0	11.5	13.7	15.7	16.7	18.2	18.0	16.0	15.9	10.6	6.0	0	7.9	17.7	29.7	43.9	60.7	80.5									
1500	7.4	10.7	13.7	16.3	18.7	20.3	21.3	21.9	21.0	19.7	16.7	12.7	6.8	0	8.7	19.3	31.7	46.6	64.6									
1600	8.7	12.7	16.0	19.1	22.0	24.3	26.3	27.0	27.2	26.0	24.0	20.4	15.3	8.7	0	9.3	21.3	34.6	50.8									
1700	10.0	14.3	18.7	22.7	26.0	29.0	31.3	32.7	33.3	33.3	32.3	29.7	25.3	18.3	10.0	0	12.6	27.6	45.9									
1800	11.3	16.7	21.3	26.0	30.3	33.8	36.7	39.0	40.3	40.7	40.0	37.7	34.3	28.7	21.3	12.0	0	14.3	32.0									
1900	13.0	19.0	24.7	30.0	35.0	39.1	43.0	46.0	48.3	49.7	49.3	48.3	45.0	40.3	33.7	25.0	14.0	0	16.8									
2000	14.3	21.3	27.7	34.0	40.0	45.1	49.7	53.3	56.7	58.3	59.3	58.7	56.7	53.0	47.3	39.3	29.0	16.0	0	18.7								
2100	16.3	24.3	31.7	38.7	45.3	51.7	57.0	62.0	65.7	67.7	70.0	70.7	69.8	66.7	62.0	54.7	45.7	33.7	18.7	0	20.7							
2200	18.3	27.3	35.7	43.7	51.3	58.3	64.7	71.0	75.3	78.7	81.0	83.7	83.7	81.7	77.7	71.7	63.3	52.3	38.5	20.7	0							
2300	20.7	30.7	40.0	49.3	58.7	66.7	74.7	82.0	89.3	94.0	98.0	98.0	99.0	98.3	95.7	90.7	83.3	73.7	60.7	44.3	24.0	0						
2400	23.0	34.0	45.0	55.3	65.3	74.7	83.3	91.7	99.0	105	110	114	115	116	115	113	109	105	96.0	84.3	70.7	53.7	30.1	0				
2500	25.7	38.0	50.0	62.0	73.3	84.0	94.3	104	112	120	126	131	134	135	136	134	132	129	125	117	108	94.7	75.7	44.0	0			
2600	28.7	42.7	56.3	69.3	82.3	94.3	106	117	127	135	143	150	153	158	158	158	158	155	149	140	131	111	91.0	58.1	27.3	0		
2700	31.7	47.7	62.7	77.7	93.0	108	119	132	143	153	163	171	178	183	185	186	184	180	172									
2800	35.3	52.7	69.7	86.3	102	119	133	147	161	173	184	194	202	209	213	215	215	212	207	197	185	168	146	119	86.0	46.8	0	
L.S.	·7	1.0	1.3	1.7	2.0	2.3	2.7	3.0	3.3	4.0	4.7	5.3	6.0	6.7	7.3	8.0	8.7	9.3	10.0	13.3	16.7	20.0	25.0	30.0	35.0	41.7		

NOTES.

The table is divided into two parts, one below the zero line and the other above. That part below the zero line is the ordinary trajectory table; that part above and the words "positive" and "negative" are for use when determining clearance in Indirect Overhead Fire. See Section 30, para. 4 (d).

PART BELOW ZERO LINE.

1.—This table gives at any distance from the gun the height IN YARDS of the centre of the cone ABOVE the line of sight.

EXAMPLE.—At a range of 1900 yards and at a distance of 1000 yards from the gun the centre of the cone is 48.3 yards above the line of sight.

2.—To find the height of the lowest shot above the line of sight, SUBTRACT the figure in the line marked L.S. from the height of the trajectory.

EXAMPLE.—At a range of 1800 yards the lowest shot at 900 yards from the gun is 39 − 3 = 36 yards above the line of sight.

PART ABOVE ZERO LINE.

1.—This table gives at any distance from the gun the height IN YARDS of the centre of the cone BELOW a horizontal plane passing through the gun position. When using this table the range is not the range to the target, but is the quadrant angle on the gun converted to a range by Table 1, column 2.

EXAMPLE.—At a range of 800 yards, and at a distance of 1200 yards from the gun the centre of the cone is 15 yards below the horizontal plane through the gun position.

2.—To find the height of the lowest s ot below the horizontal plane passing through the gun position AND the figure in the line L.S. to the height of the trajectory.

EXAMPLE.—At a range of 800 yards, the lowest shot at 1400 yards from the gun is 39 plus 6 = 36 yards below the horizontal plane through the gun position.

APPENDIX A. TABLE 2 (B).—TRAJECTORY TABLE FOR NEGATIVE QUADRANT ANGLES.
.303 VICKERS GUN, MARK VII AMMUNITION.

NOTES.

1.—This table gives at any distance from the gun the height IN YARDS of the centre shot of the cone below a horizontal plane passing through the gun position.

2.—It is for use when determining clearance over our own troops, heads in indirect overhead fire, see Section 30, para. 4 (*b*).

3.—The line Q.E. = – 5 means that at 1000 yards, for instance, each addition of 5 minutes to the Q.E. adds 1.4 yards to the height of the trajectory.

EXAMPLE.

Q.E. = – 265 minutes ; range = 1400 yards. Trajectory height = 149 plus 2 yards for each 5 minutes added above 250.
= 149 + (¹⁵⁄₅ × 2) = 153.

Distance of Point from Gun in Yards.

Q.E. Mins.	500	600	700	800	900	1000	1100	1200	1300	1400	1500	1600	1700	1800	1900	2000
	.7	.9	1.0	1.2	1.3	1.4	1.6	1.7	1.9	2.0	2.1	2.3	2.5	2.6	2.7	2.9
–0	3.2	4.8	7.1	10.0	13.6	18.0	23.7	30.4	38.2	47.5	58.7	72.1	87.5	105	125	149
–25	6.8	9.2	12.2	15.8	20.2	25.3	31.7	39.1	47.5	57.6	69.7	83.7	99.6	118	139	163
–50	10.4	13.6	17.3	21.6	26.7	32.6	39.7	47.8	57.1	67.8	80.6	95.5	112	131	153	178
–75	14.1	17.9	22.4	27.4	33.2	39.8	47.8	56.5	66.6	78.0	91.6	107	124	144	167	192
–100	17.7	22.3	27.6	33.2	39.8	47.2	55.6	65.4	76.0	88.4	102	119	137	158	180	207
–125	21.3	26.8	32.7	38.0	46.4	54.5	63.6	74.0	85.5	98.5	113	130	149	171	194	221
–150	24.0	31.1	37.8	44.7	52.9	61.6	71.6	82.8	95.0	109	124	142	162	184	208	236
–175	28.5	35.4	42.9	50.5	59.5	68.9	79.6	91.5	104	119	135	154	174	197	222	250
–200	32.2	39.7	47.8	56.4	66.1	76.1	87.6	100	114	129	146	164	186	210	236	265
–225	35.6	44.1	52.0	62.2	72.7	83.4	95.6	109	123	139	157	177	199	223	250	279
–250	39.5	48.4	58.2	68.0	79.0	90.7	101	118	133	149	168	188	211	236	264	294
–275	42.8	52.8	63.3	73.8	85.6	98.5	113	129	146	163	183	205	228	253	281	311
–300	46.8	57.1	68.4	79.6	92.1	105	120	137	155	175	196	219	243	269	298	329
–325	50.0	61.5	73.2	85.4	98.6	113	128	144	161	180	201	223	248	275	301	
–350	54.1	65.8	78.3	91.2	105	120	136	152	171	190	212	235	261	288	325	
–375	57.2	70.2	83.4	97.0	112	127	144	161	180	200	223	246				
–400	61.3	74.5	88.5	103	118	134	152	170	189	210	234					
–425	65.0	78.9	93.6	109	125	142	160	179	199	220	244					
–450	68.6	83.2	98.7	115	131	149	168	189	208	230	255					
–475	72.2	87.6	104	120	138	156	176	196	218	240						
–500	75.9	92.1	109	126	145	163	184	205	227							
–525	79.5	96.5	114	132	151	170										
–530	83.1	101	119	138	158	178										

APPENDIX A. TABLE 3 (A).—THE QUADRANT ANGLE IN MINUTES, KNOWING RANGE AND V.I. .303 VICKERS GUN, MARK VII AMMUNITION.

V.I. in Yards.	Range to Target in Yards.																						
	500	600	700	800	900	1000	1100	1200	1300	1400	1500	1600	1700	1800	1900	2000	2100	2200	2300	2400	2500	2600	2700	2800
	7	6	5	4	4	3	3	3	3	2	2	2	2	2	2	2	2	2	1	1	1	1	1	1
5	56	57	80	65	71	79	80	100	114	129	147	166	187	211	236	265	296	330	368	408	454	503	557	616
10	91	85	84	86	90	96	104	115	127	142	158	177	197	220	245	273	304	338	375	415	461	509	564	622
15	125	114	109	108	109	114	120	129	141	154	169	187	207	230	254	282	313	345	382	423	468	516	570	628
20	160	143	133	129	129	131	136	143	154	166	181	198	218	239	263	290	321	353	397	430	475	522	577	635
25	194	171	158	151	148	148	151	158	167	178	192	209	228	249	272	299	329	361	397	437	481	529	583	641
30	228	200	183	172	167	165	166	172	181	194	208	225	243	263	286	308	337	369	405	444	488	536	589	647
35	263	229	207	194	184	182	182	186	194	204	217	231	248	268	290	315	345	377	412	451	495	542	596	653
40	297	258	232	215	205	200	200	201	207	215	227	241	258	278	300	325	354	385	420	458	502	549	602	659
45	332	286	256	237	224	217	214	215	220	228	238	252	268	287	309	334	362	392	427	465	509	556	608	665
50	366	315	281	258	243	234	229	229	233	240	250	263	278	297	318	342	370	400	435	473	516	562	615	672
55	400	344	305	279	262	251	245	244	247	252	261	273	288	306	327	351	378	408	442	480	523	569	621	678
60	435	372	330	301	281	268	261	258	260	265	273	284	299	316	336	359	386	416	450	487	530	576	628	684
65	469	400	354	323	300	285	276	272	273	277	284	295	309	325	345	368	394	424	457	494	537	582	634	690
70	503	429	379	344	319	303	292	287	286	289	296	306	319	335	353	376	402	432	465	501	544	589	640	696
75	538	458	403	366	338	320	307	302	300	302	307	316	329	344	362	385	411	440	472	509	550	596	646	703
80	572	486	428	387	358	337	323	317	313	314	319	327	339	354	372	394	419	448	480	516	557	603	652	709
85	606	515	452	408	377	354	339	331	327	327	330	338	349	363	381	403	427	456	487	523	564	609	659	715
90	641	544	477	429	396	371	354	346	340	339	342	348	359	373	390	411	436	464	495	530	571	616	665	721
95	675	572	502	451	415	389	370	360	353	351	353	359	370	383	399	420	444	471	502	538	577	622	671	727
100	688	602	526	472	434	406	386	375	366	363	364	370	379	392	408	429	452	479	510	545	584	629	678	733

NOTES.

1.—This table combines the angle of sight with the angle of tangent elevation, thereby producing the quadrant angle directly.
2.—It is used as follows :—Range = 1900 yards. Target 55 yards above gun. Quadrant elevation = 327 minutes.
  EXAMPLE I : Range = 1900, V.I. = 57 yards. The quadrant elevation for range = 1900 and V.I. = 55 is 327 minutes. For each extra yard of V.I. the top line shows that 2 minutes must be ADDED. Therefore necessary quadrant angle is 327 plus (2 × 2) = 331 minutes.
3.—The top line where V.I = 1 yard is used as follows :—

APPENDIX A. TABLE 3 (B).—THE QUADRANT ANGLE IN MINUTES, KNOWING RANGE AND V.I. ·303 VICKERS GUN, MARK VII AMMUNITION.

V.I. in yards.	Range to Target in Yards.																								
	500	600	700	800	900	1000	1100	1200	1300	1400	1500	1600	1700	1800	1900	2000	2100	2200	2300	2400	2500	2600	2700	2800	
1	7	6	5	4	4	3	3	3	3	2	2	2	2	2	2	2	2	2	1	1	1	1	1	1	1
5	−12	−1	10	21	33	45	57	72	88	105	123	144	167	191	218	248	280	314	352	394	440	489	545	604	
10	−47	−29	−14	0	14	28	42	57	73	92	112	133	157	182	209	239	272	306	345	387	433	483	538	598	
15	−81	−58	−39	−22	−5	10	26	43	61	80	101	123	147	172	200	230	263	299	338	379	426	476	532	592	
20	−116	−87	−64	−43	−22	−7	10	29	48	68	90	114	139	165	193	223	257	293	330	372	420	470	525	585	
25	−150	−115	−88	−65	−43	−24	−4	15	35	56	79	102	128	153	182	212	245	281	323	365	413	463	519	579	
30	−184	−144	−113	−86	−63	−41	−21	0	21	43	66	90	116	144	173	204	236	275	315	358	406	456	513	573	
35	−219	−173	−137	−108	−82	−59	−37	−14	8	31	55	80	106	134	164	196	231	267	308	351	399	450	506	567	
40	−253	−202	−162	−129	−101	−76	−52	−29	−5	19	43	69	96	124	155	187	222	259	300	344	392	443	500	561	
45	−288	−230	−186	−151	−120	−93	−68	−43	−18	6	32	58	86	115	146	178	214	252	293	336	385	436	494	555	
50	−322	−259	−211	−172	−139	−110	−83	−57	−31	−6	20	47	76	105	137	170	206	244	285	329	378	430	487	548	
55	−357	−288	−235	−193	−158	−127	−99	−72	−45	−18	9	37	66	96	128	161	198	236	278	322	371	423	481	542	
60	−391	−316	−260	−215	−177	−144	−115	−86	−58	−31	−3	26	55	86	119	153	189	228	260	315	364	416	474	536	
65	−425	−344	−284	−237	−197	−161	−130	−100	−71	−43	−14	15	45	77	110	144	181	220	263	308	358	410	468	530	
70	−460	−372	−309	−258	−216	−179	−146	−115	−84	−55	−26	5	35	67	101	136	173	212	255	301	351	403	462	524	
75	−495	−401	−333	−280	−235	−196	−161	−129	−97	−67	−37	−6	25	57	92	128	166	206	248	294	344	397	456	518	
80	−529	−430	−358	−301	−254	−214	−177	−144	−111	−79	−48	−17	15	48	82	119	158	199	240	287	337	391	449	512	
85	−563	−459	−382	−323	−273	−231	−192	−158	−124	−92	−60	−28	5	38	73	111	140	191	233	280	330	384	443	506	
90	−598	−488	−407	−344	−292	−248	−208	−172	−137	−104	−71	−39	−5	29	64	102	141	183	225	273	323	378	436	500	
95	−632	−517	−431	−366	−311	−265	−223	−186	−150	−117	−83	−50	−15	19	55	93	132	175	218	266	316	371	430	494	
100	−666	−545	−456	−387	−330	−282	−239	−200	−163	−129	−94	−60	−25	10	46	85	124	167	210	259	310	365	424	488	

NOTES.

1.—This table combines the angle of sight with the angle of tangent elevation, thereby producing the quadrant angle directly.
2.—It is used as follows:—Range = 1000 yards. Target 55 yards below gun. Quadrant elevation = 128 minutes.
3.—The top line where V.I. = 1 yard is used as follows:—EXAMPLE I: Range = 1900 yards. Target 57 yards below gun. The quadrant angle for range = 1900 and V.I. = 55 is 128 minutes. For each extra yard of V.I. the top line shows that 2 minutes must be SUBTRACTED. Therefore necessary quadrant angle is 128 − (2 × 2) = 124 minutes. EXAMPLE II: Range = 1300 yards, V.I. = 38 yards, Q.E. = 8 − (3 × 3) = −1 minute. EXAMPLE III: Range = 1100 yards, V.I. = 47 yards, Q.E. = − 68 − (2 × 3) = − 74 minutes.

APPENDIX A. TABLE 4.—WIND ALLOWANCES.

The following is the usual table for rough guidance:—

Yards.	Lateral Allowances.					
	Mild.		Fresh.		Strong.	
	Yards.	Minutes.	Yards.	Minutes.	Yards.	Minutes.
500 ...	1	5	1½	10	2	15
1000 ...	3	10	6	20	9	20
1500 ...	6	15	12	30	18	45
2000 ...	12	20	24	40	36	60

NOTES.

(i) The table is for right angle winds; halve the allowances for oblique winds.

(ii) The minutes of angle should be used in conjunction with a card and string in order to obtain an auxiliary aiming mark on which to order the gunner to lay.

(iii) When no clearly defined auxiliary mark is obtainable the lateral angular allowance may be put on by the direction dial, if the angle is reasonably large. If not, the following rough rule may prove of value.

(iv) Assume the following factors:—Mild, 2; Fresh, 3; Strong, 4; then multiply the range by the appropriate factor, and the first figure of the answer gives the taps required. Thus fresh wind at 1500 yards; $1500 \times 3 = 4500$; 4 taps are necessary.

(v) The deflection due to drift is negligible below 1000 yards. At 1500 yards it is about 2 yards. Above 1500 yards it is unknown but is certainly several yards at extreme ranges.

N.B.—Drift is to the left.

TABLE 6.
TIME OF FLIGHT.

Total time of flight in seconds.	Distance covered in yards.
1	600
2	1000
3	1300
4	1550
5	1775
6	1950
7	2100
8	2225
9	2350
10	2450
11	2550
12	2625
13	2700
14	2775
15	2840

TABLE 5.
ALLOWANCES FOR ATMOSPHERIC INFLUENCES.

More Elevation.	Less Elevation.
Cold (40° Fahrenheit or less). Strong Head Wind. Extreme Dryness.	Heat (80° Fahrenheit or more). Strong Rear Wind. Rain. Over 3000 feet above sea.

ALLOWANCES IN YARDS OF RANGE.

Range.	1 Factor.	2 Factors.
1000 yards	—	50
1500 "	50	100
2000 "	100	150

NOTES.

(i) Due to the effect of light on the human eye, *more* elevation must be given in a very bright light and *less* elevation in a very poor light.

(ii) Factors affecting elevation in opposite directions will naturally cancel out; the result of combined factors only must be used in the allowance table.

(iii) Less elevation is required when firing up or down hill. This may be neglected when the angle of sight to the target does not exceed 10°.

APPENDIX A. TABLE 7.—SEARCHING REVERSE SLOPES ·303 VICKERS GUN. MARK VII AMMUNITION.

All figures represent yards.

Notes.

1.—The top horizontal line is the drop IN YARDS in the first 100 yards beyond the crest. The horizontal line directly below it is the distance to measure back from the crest to find gun position.

2.—For full explanation of use of table, see Section 31.

EXAMPLE.—The ground drops 7 yards in 100, and assume also that the gun is below the crest. The left-hand side of table must therefore be used. The table shows that for a drop of 7 yards we must go back 1000 yards from the crest. At this point, say, the gun position is found to be 90 yards below the crest. Final range, therefore, equals 2000 yards. Place the gun at this point.

3.—When the gun is in position, fire should be directed on the crest, elevation and direction being put on by any of the usual methods for indirect fire. In the example given above, the quadrant angle is that for a V.I. of 90 yards and a range of 2000 yards—i.e., 411 minutes. See Table 3 (A).

4.—Searching should be employed away from the crest, but it must be remembered that as the cone is beating falling ground the length of the zone will be very much increased; therefore the turns of the wheel should be few in number.

5.—If the final position is not suitable the gun should be moved further away from—not nearer to—the crest, and the elevation increased by the distance moved.

6.—If it be desired to engage an area of ground which lies some distance back from the crest, without searching back from the crest itself, the position of the gun must be determined with reference to the crest as detailed above. Then the quadrant elevation necessary to hit the near limit of the ground to be searched must be put on in the usual way for indirect fire.

Gun BELOW Crest

1	2	3	4	5	6	7	8	9	10	11	12	Gun Above or Below Crest.
											2100	0
										2050	2100	10
									2000	2050	2100	20
								1950	2000	2050	2100	30
							1900	1950	2000	2050	2100	40
						1850	1900	1950	2000	2050	2100	50
					1800	1850	1900	1950	2000	2050	2150	60
				1750	1800	1850	1900	1950	2050	2100	2150	70
				1750	1800	1850	1900	2000	2050	2100	2150	80
				1750	1800	1850	1950	2000	2050	2150	2200	90
			1800	1850	1900	1950	2000	2100	2150	2200	2200	100
			1800	1850	1900	1950	2050	2100	2150	2200	2200	110
			1850	1900	2000	2050	2100	2150	2200	2250	2250	120
		1850	1900	1950	2000	2050	2150	2200	2250	2250	2250	130
		1900	1950	2000	2050	2100	2150	2200	2250	2300	2300	140
		1950	2000	2050	2100	2150	2200	2250	2300	2300	2300	150
	2000	2050	2100	2150	2200	2250	2300	2300	2300		160
	2050	2100	2150									170
2100	2150											180
2200	2250											190
2250												200

Gun ABOVE Crest

12	11	10	9	8	7	6	5	4	3	2	1
1900	1800	1700	1600	1500	1400	1400	1350	1300	1300	1300	1200
2050	2000	1950	1900	1850	1800	1700	1650	1600	1500	1400	1350
2000	1950	1900	1850	1800	1750	1650	1600	1550	1450	1300	1150
2000	1950	1900	1850	1800	1700	1650	1550	1450	1350	1200	
1950	1900	1850	1800	1750	1650	1600	1500	1400	1250	1100	
1900	1850	1800	1750	1700	1600	1500	1450	1300	1150		
1900	1850	1750	1700	1600	1550	1450	1350	1200			
1850	1800	1700	1600	1450	1400	1350	1300				
1800	1750	1650	1550	1400	1300	1300	1200				
1750	1700	1600	1500	1350	1250	1150					
1750	1700	1600	1450	1250	1150						
1700	1650	1550	1400	1200	1150						
1650	1600	1500	1350	1150							
1600	1550	1450	1300	1100							
1600	1550	1450	1250								
1550	1500	1400	1200								
1500	1450	1330	1150								
1450	1400	1300									
1400	1350	1250									
1400	1350										
1350	1300										
1300											

88

APPENDIX B.—INDIRECT OVERHEAD FIRE SHEET.

No. 515 M.G. Coy. No. 3 Section. Date, 11.2.19. Map used, 36c N.W. 3. 1/10,000. Officer i/c Firing, 2/Lt. D. Hay.

Gun No.	Target.	Elevation.						Clearance Over Own Troops.					Direction.			Remarks.		
		Range to Target in Yards.	Contours in Yards.		V.I. in Yards.	Q.E. Minutes. Table 3 (A) or 3 (B).	Range for Q.E. in Yards, Table 1, Col. 2.	Contour of Own Troops in Yards. B.	Range to Own Troops in Yards.	Trajectory Height in Yards. Table 2 (A) or 2 (B).	Clearance obtained by Note(1) below in Yards.	Clearance required in Yards.	Compass Bearing D.D. Reading.	Time of Firing.	Number of Rounds Fired.	Checked by—	General.
			Gun A.	Target.													
1	Dump, U.28.b.5.4.	2,000	118	93	25	213	1,850	104	400	23 Positive	37	20	80° magnetic	19.56	500	D.H.	Traversed and searched slightly. Enemy retaliated on front line with 77 mm. Shells.
2	Brickworks, U.29.c.0.9	1,900	100	140	40	300	2,150	—	—	—	—	—	D.D. 62° (left of R.O.)	10.00 & 12.24	750	D.H.	Own troops not between gun and target. Artillery F.O.O. reports enemy casualties on both occasions.
3	Cross roads, B.17.d.5.1.	1,500	111	63	47	28	600	88	700	1 Negative	22	20	D.D. 72°–74° (right of R.O.)	21.15	355	D.H.	Firing line reports noises of stampeding transport. Enemy retaliated on dummy emplacement.
4	Battalion Headquarters, B.18.a.8.4	1,700	132	29	103	−31	—	114	550	9 Negative	0	20	71° magnetic	—	—	D.H.	Insufficient clearance over own troops. Did not fire.
5 to 10	Barrage on near edge of Crow Wood	2,300	111 Lowest	138	27	299	2,300	95	1,100	105 Positive	121	40	Parallel lines of fire 101° magnetic	On call from infantry	41,500	D.H. L.T.V. R.O.A.	S.O.S. signal at 18.20, 19.30, 19.56 and 21.10. No enemy attacks developed.
3	Shafskopf Redoubt	2,200	119	71	48	258	2,000	99 & 97	900 & 1,500	53 & 53 Both Positive	73 & 75	20 & 40	Gun laid by day.	19.08	710	D.H.	Traversed slightly. No information as to results.

NOTES.

1.—CLEARANCE in yards = A − B plus or minus C according as trajectory tables give positive or negative values of C.
2.—IMMEDIATELY before firing, Q.E. must be corrected, if necessary, for atmospheric influences, see Table 5.
3.—For lateral wind allowance see Table 4.
4.—If obstruction exists between gun and target and its highest point cannot be seen, ascertain if shots will clear by substituting "Obstruction" for "Own Troops" in clearance columns above and find clearance by rule. NOTE.—Minimum clearance required is one-half height of cone at range to obstruction.

KEY TO PLATES.

♁	....	Company Commander.
☥	....	Second in Command.
☥	....	Section Officer.
☥	....	Sub-section Officer.
♁	....	Company Serjeant-Major.
⊡	....	Company Quarter Master Serjeant
⊡	....	Serjeant.
C	....	Corporal.
R	....	Range Taker.
S	....	Scout.
1	....	Gun Number, Lance Corporal or **Private.**
A	....	Artificer.
B	....	Batman.
Sd	....	Saddler.
Sh	....	Shoeingsmith.
Ck	....	Cook.
Sr	....	Storeman.
⊠	....	Driver.
Sg	....	Signaller.
F	....	Filterer.
0	....	Horse or Mule.

PLATE I.
Machine Gun Company drawn up in Line.

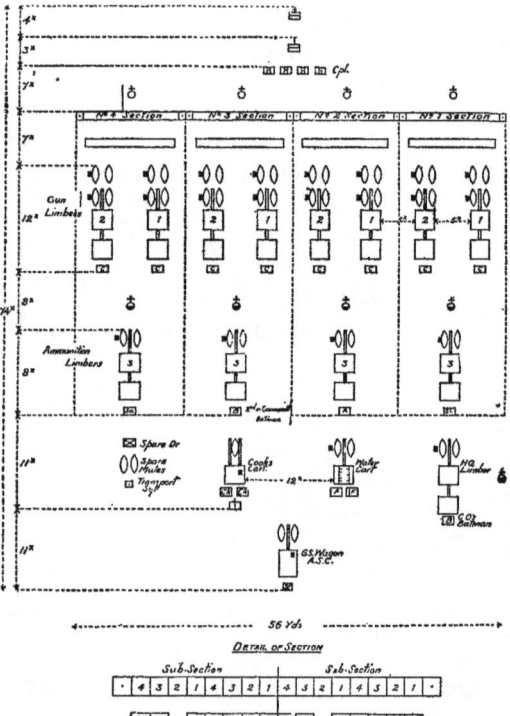

PLATE II.

Machine Gun Company in column of route.
Action not expected.

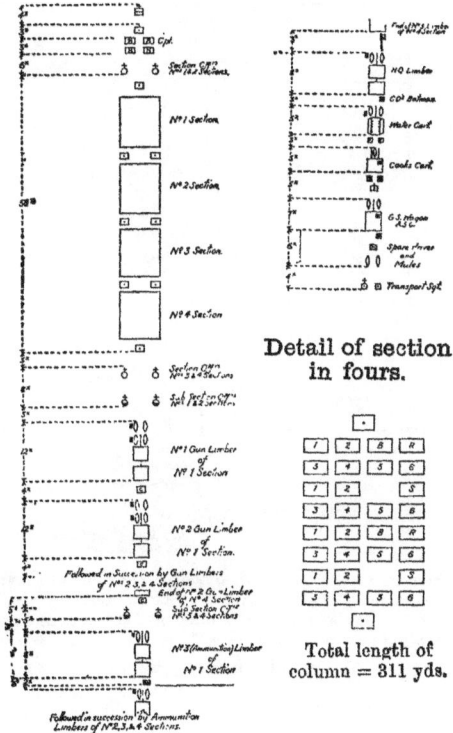

Detail of section in fours.

Total length of column = 311 yds.

PLATE III.
Machine Gun Company in column of route.
Action expected.

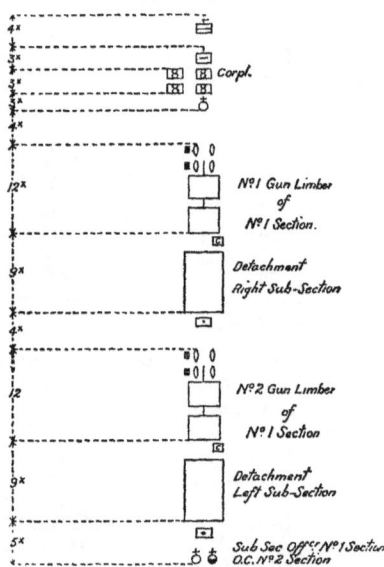

Followed in succession by 2, 3 and 4 Sections in above order. The Sub-section Officer of No. 4 Section followed by No. 3 (Ammunition) Limbers and remainder of Transport in same order as shown when action is not expected.

Length of column = 326 yds.

PLATE IV.

Mounting Gun at Elementary Drill.

Points to note :—

1. Method of supporting gun on the right thigh by No. 2.
2. Forcing crosshead joint pin home with handle upwards.
3. Firm grip with left hand on rear crosspiece.
4. No. 1 assisting with left hand.
5. No. 1 ready to connect elevating screw to the bracket with right hand.

PLATE V.

Gun incorrectly mounted.

Points to note :—
- *Tripod*—1. Feet not firmly planted in ground.
  2. Rear leg at an angle to the line of fire.
  3. Socket inclined.
  4. Joint pin not turned down.
  5. Upper elevating screw too short.
- *Gun*—1. Inclined to one side.
  2. Muzzle pointing upwards.
  3. Condenser tube outside front carrying handle.

PLATE VI.

Points to note:— **Normal Firing Position (Sitting).**
1. Gun and Tripod mounted correctly at suitable height, with belt box in position.
2. Condenser tube passed through the loop of front carrying handle.
3. Condenser bag screened as far as possible.
4. *No. 1.*—Feet closed in and firmly planted in ground.
5. Correct method of taking "holding" pressure with both hands.
6. Elbows supported inside the thighs.   7. Eyes directed towards the target.
8. *No. 2.*—Lowest possible position.   9. Right hand assisting feed belt.
10. Observing controlling officer from position below the gun.
11. Left hand out horizontally indicating "Ready to fire."

PLATE VII.

Normal Firing Position (Lying).

Points to note :—

1. Gun and Tripod mounted in lowest position with socket clear of the ground.
2. No. 1.—Heels firm on ground and legs close in to gun.
3. "Holding" pressure taken with both hands, arms close to body.
4. Back supported by No. 2.
5. No. 2.—Lowest possible position consistent with performance of duties.
6. Right hand keeping ammunition box in position.
7. Watching for signals from a position below the gun.
8. Left hand out indicating "Gun ready to fire."
9. Knees drawn up behind No. 1 for support.

PLATE VIII.

Points to note:— **Mounting Gun (Vickers) in prone position.**
1. Minimum exposure.
2. Tripod mounted in lowest position—socket just clear of ground.
3. *No. 1.*—Position taken up on left of gun.
4. Left hand supporting barrel casing.
5. Right hand forcing home the crosshead joint pin.
6. *No. 2.*—Left hand gripping rear crosspiece.
7. Ready to connect elevating screw to the bracket with right hand.

PLATE IX.

Firing with Auxiliary Tripod.

Points to note :—

1. Feet of tripod forced in ground by No. 2.
2. Sights upright.
3. *No. 1.*—Correct "holding" with both hands.
4. Elbows splayed out to support gun and body.
5. *No. 2.*—Assisting feed belt with right hand.
6. Left hand out indicating "Gun ready to fire."
7. Watching controlling officer.

PLATE X.

Points to note :— **Positions when firing along a steep slope.**
Tripod.—1. Feet firmly planted. Legs adjusted to suit ground. Rear leg down the slope.
2. Socket upright.
Gun.—3. Loaded and laid correctly. 4. Condenser tube inside carrying handle.
No. 1.—5. Position suitable to ground. 6. Holding pressure, supported by No. 2.
No. 2.—7. Supporting ammunition box with right hand.
8. Watching controlling officer. 9. Hand out indicating "Gun ready to fire."

PLATE XI.

Positions when firing down a steep slope.

Points to note:—
Tripod.—1. Legs adjusted to suit ground.   2. Socket upright.
Gun.—3. Loaded and laid.   Rear leg down slope.   4. Condenser tube Inside carrying handle.
No. 1.—5. Position adapted to suit ground.   6. "Holding" with arms close to body.
No. 2.—7. Supporting ammunition box.   8. Position adapted to ground.

PLATE XII.

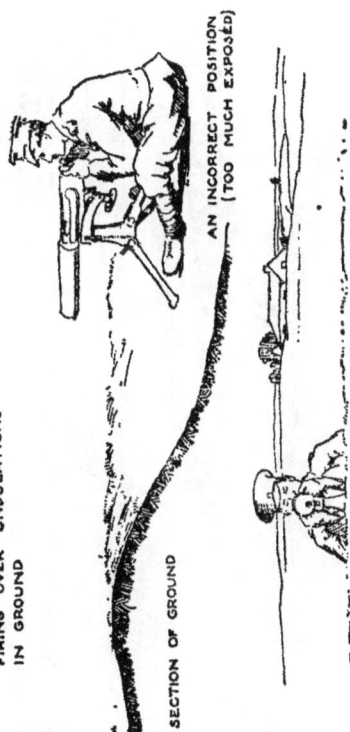

PLATE XIII.

PLATE XIV.

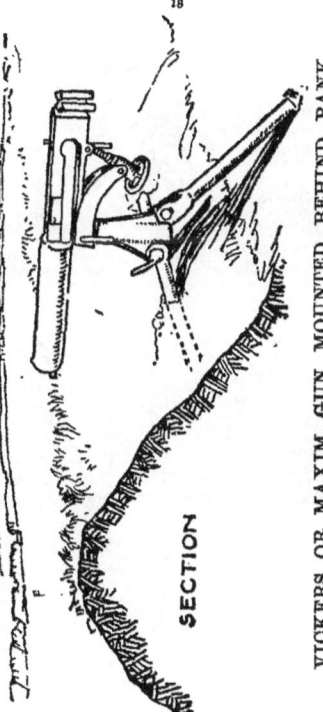

VICKERS OR MAXIM GUN MOUNTED BEHIND BANK.

PLATE XV.

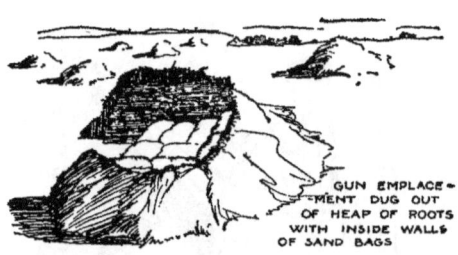

GUN EMPLACE-
MENT DUG OUT
OF HEAP OF ROOTS
WITH INSIDE WALLS
OF SAND BAGS

STACK OF WOOD USED AS
GUN EMPLACEMENT.

PLATE XVI.

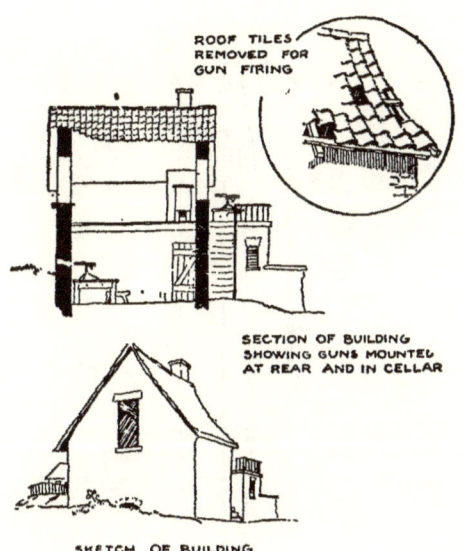

ROOF TILES REMOVED FOR GUN FIRING

SECTION OF BUILDING SHOWING GUNS MOUNTED AT REAR AND IN CELLAR

SKETCH OF BUILDING

PLATE XVII.

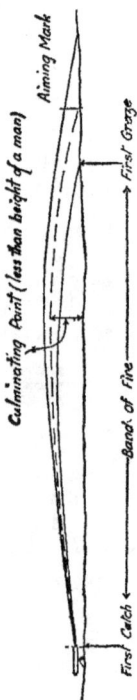

PLATE XVIII.

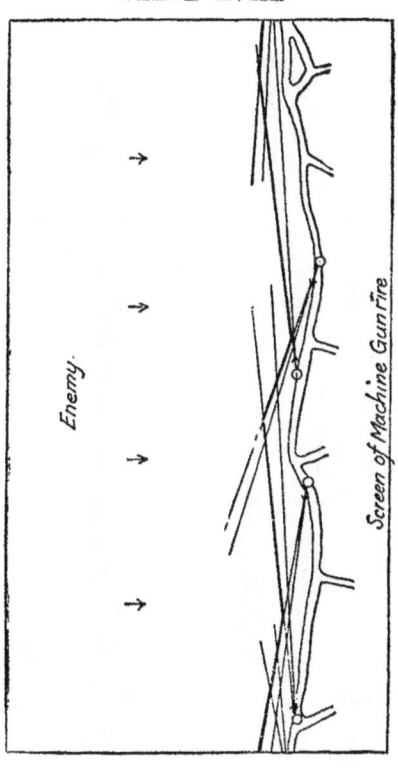

PLATE XIX.

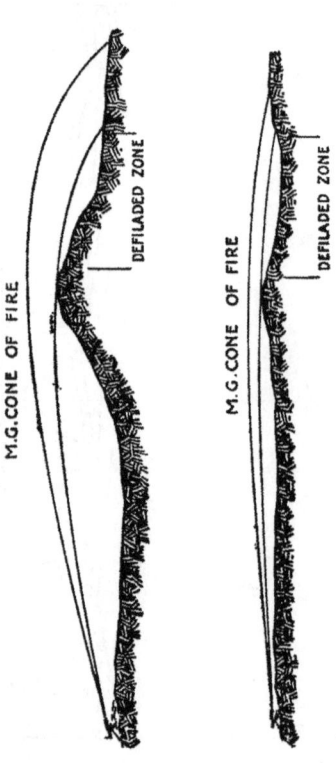

PLATE XX.

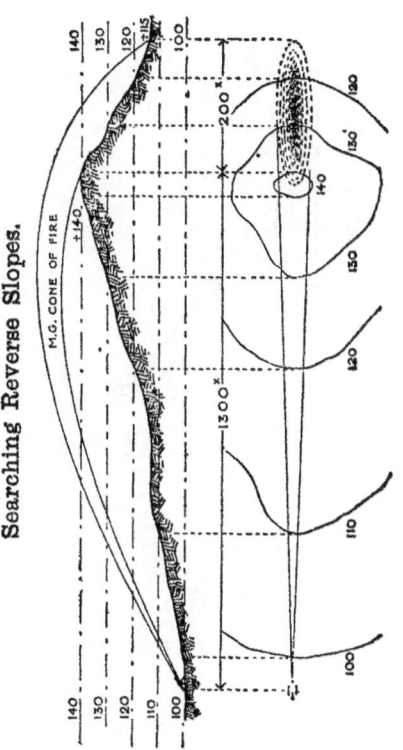

Searching Reverse Slopes.

PLATE XXI.

Use of Combined Sights.

PLATE XXII.

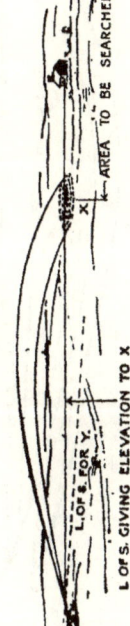

Searching Fire.

PLATE XXIII.

Searching Fire. Using Two Guns.

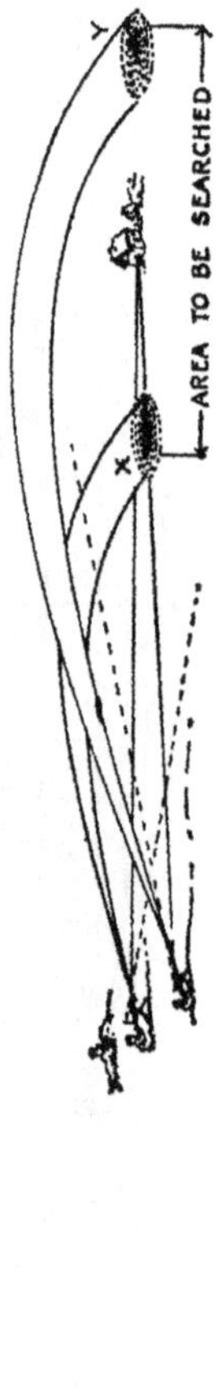

PLATE XXIV.

Overhead Fire—Protractor Method.

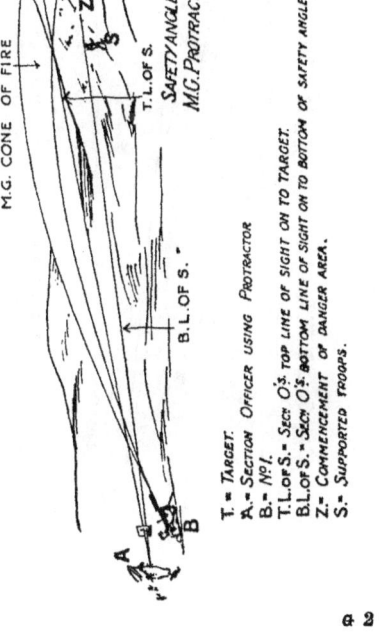

T. = TARGET.
A. = SECTION OFFICER USING PROTRACTOR
B. = N°1.
T.L. OF S. = SECN O'S. TOP LINE OF SIGHT ON TO TARGET.
B.L. OF S. = SECN O'S. BOTTOM LINE OF SIGHT ON TO BOTTOM OF SAFETY ANGLE AT Z.
Z. = COMMENCEMENT OF DANGER AREA.
S. = SUPPORTED TROOPS.

PLATE XXV.

Overhead Fire—Tangent Sight Method.

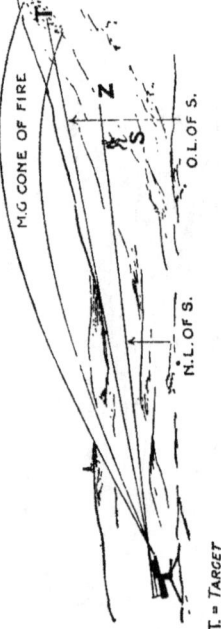

T. = TARGET
O. L OF S. = ORIGINAL LINE OF SIGHT ON TARGET WITH CORRECT ELEVATION ON GUN
N. L. OF S. = NEW LINE OF SIGHT ON TO BOTTOM OF SAFETY ANGLE AT Z
S. = SUPPORTED TROOPS.

PLATE XXVI.

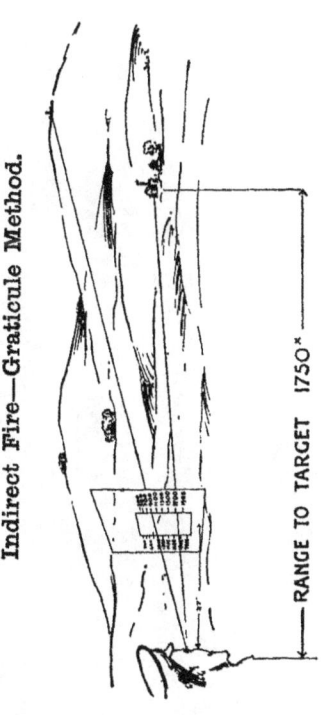

Indirect Fire—Graticule Method.

RANGE TO TARGET 1750×

[*Crown Copyright Reserved.*

[FOR OFFICIAL USE ONLY.]

MACHINE-GUN SQUADRON DRILL.

(*Issued as an Addendum to " Machine Gun Training."*)

To be read in conjunction with " Cavalry Training, 1912 (1915).

ISSUED BY THE GENERAL STAFF.

February, 1918.

LONDON:
Printed under the Authority of His Majesty's Stationery Office
By HARRISON & SONS, 45–47, St. Martin's Lane, W.C. 2,
Printers in Ordinary to His Majesty.

CONTENTS.

Chapter I.—*Organization and Definitions.*

SEC.		PAGE.
1.	Organization	3
2.	Definitions	3
3.	Terms of formation	4
4.	Intervals and distances	5

Chapter II.—*Allocation of Duties.*

5.	Allocation of Duties	6

Chapter III.—*Mounted Drill for a Machine-Gun Squadron.*

6.	General instructions	8
7.	Post of officers, N.C.Os., &c.	8
8.	Detachment drill	9
9.	Sub-section drill	11
10.	Section drill	16
11.	Squadron drill	20
12.	Going into action	22
13.	Action	24
14.	Advancing and retiring after action	24

PLATES.

I.	Symbols	26
II.	Column of Sub-sections	27
III.	Section drill. (Column of detachments)	28
IV.	Section drill. (Line of detachment column)	29
V.	Section drill. (Sub-section in "Column of route" or "Advance by Files")	30
VI.	Section drill. (Sub-section in "Detachment column")	31
VII.	Squadron drill. ("Line of detachment column")	32
VIII.	Squadron drill. (Column of Detachments. Column of Sub-sections)	33
IX.	Machine-Gun Squadron. (Drawn up for Inspection)	34
X.	Squadron drill. (Mass)	35
XI.	A Sub-section of a Machine-Gun Squadron in action	36

CHAPTER I.

ORGANIZATION AND DEFINITIONS.

1.—ORGANISATION.

1. *A Machine-Gun Squadron* consists of Headquarters and 3 sections each of 4 guns. *A Section* consists of 2 sub-sections. *A sub-section* consists of 2 detachments.

2. *A detachment* consists of the gun numbers and pack leaders detailed for the service of one gun under the immediate control of a N.C.O. called the detachment leader.

3. The machine guns of a section are carried on pack animals. Each sub-section has one limbered G.S. wagon for ammunition.

4. Further details as to personnel, horses and vehicles are given in War Establishments.

2.—DEFINITIONS.

The following definitions are added to those given in "Cavalry Training."

File.—Two men riding abreast followed by a pack leader and pack horse.

Half File.—Two men riding abreast, *or* a pack leader and pack horse.

Detachment.—Gun teams, packs, shoeing smith, &c., formed up in three ranks.

    Front rank   ...   . Nos. 1 to 7.
    Rear rank   ...   . Packs (one gun and 2 ammunition).

Serrefile rank.—Spare pack, shoeing smith, signaller, servant and corporal.

3.—TERMS OF FORMATION.

1. *Column.*

    Column of Route.—A column of files.

    Column of Sections.—Sections in line one behind the other at wheeling distance, plus 5 yards.

    Column of Sub-Sections.—Sub-sections in line one behind the other, at wheeling distance, plus 5 yards, the sub-section leaders riding 16 feet in rear of serrefile rank of preceding sub-section.

    Column of Detachments.—Detachments in line one behind the other, at wheeling distance, detachment leaders riding 4 feet in rear of serrefile rank of preceding detachment.

    Section Column.—A section in column of detachments.

2. *Line.*

    Line of Detachment Columns.—Detachments in column of route parallel to one another at 10 yards interval. This interval can always be increased.

    Line of Section Columns.—Sections in column of detachments parallel to each other at 33 yards interval.

3. *Mass.*

    Mass.—Sections in column of detachments parallel to each other at 5 yards interval. (See plate IX.)

4.—INTERVALS AND DISTANCES.

1. *Intervals.*

Intervals are measured from wagon to wagon, and from knee to knee between files.

20 yards from wagon to wagon is full interval.
10 ,, ,, ,, ,, ,, ,, half ,,
4 ,, ,, ,, ,, ,, ,, close ,,

In Line.—Between sub-sections... ... 5 yards.
Between sections ... ... 5 yards.

In line of detachments column.—Between detachments 10 yards.

In Mass.—Between sections ... ... 5 yards.
In Line of Section Columns.—Between sections 33 yards.

NOTE.—To form line of detachment columns from line of Section columns this interval must be increased to 60 yards.

2. *Distances.*

Distances are measured between animals from tail to head, between wagons from rear end of wagons to head of the following team.

In Line.—Sub-section leaders to front rank, front to rear rank, rear rank to serrefile rank ... 1 horse length.

In Column.—Front to rear rank, rear rank to serrefile rank ... ... ½ horse length.

In Column of Sections.—Sub-section leaders to front rank ½ horse length.

In Column of Sub-sections ⎫ Sub-section leaders to front
In Column of Detachments ⎭ rank ... ½ horse length.

CHAPTER II.

5.—ALLOCATION OF DUTIES.

1. The duties of the *section commander* are to command the section in accordance with his orders and the tactical situation, to select gun positions, to observe and to control fire generally, and to regulate the ammunition supply.

2. The duties of the *sub-section officer* are to assist the section commander and to act as second in command of the section. He should be ready to replace the section commander should the latter become a casualty. Normally, he will command one sub-section in action and supervise the transport of his section in quarters and on the line of march.

3. The duties of the *detachment leaders* (1 Serjeant and 1 Corporal) are to supervise guns coming into action as the section officer may direct, and to observe and control the fire of his own gun. The serjeant must be prepared to take command of the section in the event of both the officers becoming casualties. They are responsible for replacing casualties among the gun numbers when they occur. One serjeant will be in charge of the led horses.

4. One *corporal* is responsible generally for the packing of gun equipment and contents of the ammunition limber. In the absence of the section officer or serjeant, he will take command. In action he will have the spare parts box handy, supervise the ammunition supply and filling the belts, direct the ammunition limber as required, superintend the filling of sandbags and watch for signals from the section officer. He will be prepared to take the place of the serjeant should he become a casualty.

5. The following are the duties of the various numbers:—

No. 1 is the firer. He will personally clean and look after his gun, and ensure that the mechanism is working smoothly. On going into action he will carry the Mark IV tripod and place it in a suitable position and assist No. 4 in mounting the gun. He repeats all orders received, observes his own fire when possible, and makes the necessary alterations of elevation and direction.

No. 4 assists No. 1 at the gun, carries the gun into action when No. 1 is carrying the tripod, and mounts it with the assistance of No. 1.

On going into action he will secure the tube of the condenser to the gun, and take the spare parts case. In action he will attend to the feeding of the gun, watch for signals from the section or company officer, and generally assist No. 1.

No. 3 is responsible for keeping the gun supplied with ammunition; seeing that the condenser (half-filled with water) reaches the gun position before there is any chance of the water in barrel casing boiling; and carry out minor repairs whilst the gun is in action.

No. 5 assists No. 3 in his duties. He is responsible for keeping No. 3 supplied with ammunition, water, and spare parts from the spare parts box as required.

No. 2 is horseholder, No. 6 is scout; No. 7 of left detachment is range taker; No. 7 of right detachment horseholder; No. 8 is gun pack leader; No. 9 is first ammunition leader; No. 10 is second ammunition leader; No. 11 is spare pack leader.

6. Section officers will ensure that each man of the section is thoroughly trained in the duties of each "number." A system of "changing round" will be arranged, so that every man will perform the several duties of the section in turn.

CHAPTER III.

MOUNTED DRILL FOR A MACHINE-GUN SQUADRON.

6.—GENERAL INSTRUCTIONS.

1. At drill and manœuvre, the squadron will be divided into sections.

2. Numbering in line is from right to left, in column from the right of the head of the column.

The relative positions of sections and sub-sections within a squadron or of detachments within a sub-section may be changed at any time, but sub-sections must not be broken up.

The section or sub-section on the right of the line is always, for the time being, the right section or sub-section. Line is to be formed in any required direction with the utmost rapidity, without regard to the original positions which sections or sub-sections occupied when they were last told off.

3. When it is intended to increase the front, the formation may be to either or both flanks. If no special order is given, the formation will be outwards. If it is intended to form on the right or left it must be so stated.

7.—POST OF OFFICERS, N.C.Os., &c.

The Squadron.

THE SQUADRON COMMANDER—

In Line.—One horse length in front of the centre of the line of section commanders.

While Drill is in Progress.—Wherever he can best superintend and command his squadron.

THE SQUADRON-SERJEANT-MAJOR—

In Line.—One horse length in rear of the centre of the squadron.

Supernumerary officers and N.C.Os. in rear of the squadron.

The Sub-section.

THE SUB-SECTION COMMANDER—

In Line.—One horse length in front of the centre of his sub-section.

In Column of Route.—Where he can best superintend the march discipline of his sub-section.

SERGEANTS—

In Line.—In the centre of the sub-section in line with the men of the front rank of the detachment. One in the serrefile rank.

In Column of Route.—One at the head of the sub-section and one in rear of the sub-section.

CORPORALS—

One with the ammunition wagon.

THE SECOND CORPORAL—

In Line.—In the serrefile rank.

In Column of Route.—In rear of the sub-section.

8.—DETACHMENT DRILL.

1. *Formation of the Detachment.*

The detachment will fall in in three ranks, the gun numbers in front, the pack leaders and pack horses in the rear rank, shoeing smiths, signallers, officer's grooms and spare pack horses in the serrefile rank.

The senior N.C.O. in the detachment will be posted as detachment leader half a horse length in front of No. 4. When in *line* the distance between ranks is one horse length; in *column*, half a horse length.

From the Right—Number.

Proving a Detachment.—The gun numbers number off from the right, 1 to 7. The flanks and even numbers then prove as in Cavalry Training.

2.—*Diminishing and increasing the front.*

"Form Detachment Column."

From line to detachment column.—The right file advances; the remaining files as it comes to their turn, incline to the right, follow, and cover at the proper distance.

The spare pack follows the second ammunition pack.

No. 7 and signaller, or shoeing smith, form a half file and follow the spare pack.

The detachment leader places himself in front of No. 1 and directs.

"Form Line."

From detachment column to line.—The leading file continues to advance; the remaining files incline to the left and move up at an increased pace into their places in line.

3.—*Movements to a flank.*

"Files Right."

From line to form detachment column to the right.—The right file wheels to the right and moves off, the remaining files wheel and follow in succession.

If the order is given when the detachment is moving, all but the leading file halt until it is their turn to move ; they then wheel and follow.

NOTE.—It is not possible to go *files left*. If detachment column to the left flank is wanted, the order is "**Left Wheel —Form Detachment Column.**"

"**Half Files Right,**" or "**Left.**"

To gain ground to a flank when in detachment column.— Every half file wheels to the flank named.

A further wheel to the opposite flank brings the detachment into column again moving in its original direction.

9.—SUB-SECTION DRILL.

1.—*Formations of the sub-section.*

Line.—The detachments each in line, side by side without intervals.

Column of detachments.—The detachments in column at a distance of 16 feet. (Plate III.)

Line of detachment columns.—Each detachment in column, at 10 yards interval. A useful formation for working over rough ground and into action.

The sub-section will be formed up on parade, with the two detachments in line.

The senior N.C.O. will be posted as centre guide between No. 7 of the right detachment and No. 1 of the left detachment.

The second serjeant will cover off the centre guide in the serrefile rank.

The sub-section leader will take post one horse length in front of the centre guide *in line*, half horse length in *column*.

"From the right tell off by Detachments."

Proving a Sub-section.—The gun numbers of each detachment numbers off from the right, 1 to 7. The flanks and even numbers then move as in Cavalry Training.

2.—*Diminishing the front.*

"Form Column of Route."

From line to column of route.—Nos. 1 and 2 followed by gun pack and leader of right detachment advance, serjeant and groom forming a half file and directing.

Nos. 3 and 4 followed by first ammunition pack and leader incline to right, follow and cover.

Nos. 5 and 6 followed by second ammunition pack and leader incline to the right, follow and cover.

Spare pack follows and covers.

No. 7 and signaller form a half file, follow and cover.

Left detachment acts in a like manner, except that No. 7 and shoeing smith form a half file. The serjeant and corporal bring up the rear.

"Advance in " or " Form Column of Detachments."

From line to column of detachments.—The right detachment advances.

The sub-section leader places himself in front of No. 4 and leads to the front.

Left detachment inclines to the right, follows and covers.

Serjeant places himself in front of No. 4 and rides at 4 feet from serrefile rank of leading detachment.

3.—*Increasing the front.*

" Form Line."

From column of route to line.—As in Section 8 (2).

" Form Sub-section."

From column of detachment to line.—The right detachment continues at the original pace, the left detachment inclines to the left, and moves up at an increased pace into line.

4.—*Formations used for moving across country and into action.*

" Form (Line of) Detachment Column." (Plate IV.)

From line to detachment column.—Each detachment forms column as in Section 8 (2).

The serjeant takes post in front of No. 1 of left detachment and directs.

The Corporal takes post in rear of right detachment.

The second serjeant takes post in front of No. 1 and 2 respectively of right detachment.

The sub-section leader takes post one horse length in front of, and half-way between, the leading files of the two detachments.

The left detachment directs : the right detachment inclines outwards to 10 yards interval from the left detachment.

" Form line of Detachment Column."

From column of detachments to line of detachment columns.—The leading detachment forms detachment column and directs. The rear detachment forms detachment column and is led at an increased pace into line with, and at 10 yards interval from, the directing detachment.

5.—*Formations and movements to a flank and rear.*

" Right (Left) Wheel into Line."

From column of detachments to form line to a flank.—Each detachment wheels to the flank named, on completing the wheel, the left detachment right inclines and closes in upon the right detachment.

The serjeant takes post as centre guide.

The sub-section leader takes post one horse length in front of centre guide.

" Form Column of Detachments to the Right " (Left)
" Detachments Right (Left) Wheel."

From line, to form column of detachments to a flank.—The right (left) detachment wheels to the flank named; the remaining detachment waits, and if on the move, halts, until its flank is clear, then wheels and follows.

" Files Right."

From column of detachments to form line of detachment columns to the right.—As in (4). Note that the interval between detachment column in line will be 16 yards.

" Half Files Right (Left)."

To gain ground to a flank when in line of detachment column.—As in Section 8 (3).

" Detachments Right (Left) about Wheel."

From line, and from column of detachments, to go about. Each detachment wheels about as in Cavalry Drill.

" Right (Left) about Wheel."

From line of detachment columns, to go about.—Each detachment wheels about on its own head.

6.—*From line of detachment column.*

"**Form Sub-section.**"

To form sub-section.—Each detachment forms line.

The left detachment continues to advance and directs; the right detachment closes in upon the left detachment.

Sub-section leader and centre guide take post.

"**Form Column of Detachments from the Right (Left).**"

To form column of detachments from a named flank.—Each detachment forms into line.

The right (left) detachment advances; the other right (or left) inclines, follows and covers.

7.—*Dismounting for action.*

"**For Action Dismount.**"

The formation in which to dismount for action is line of detachment column.

No. 1 hands his horse over to No. 2.

No. 4 moves up abreast of No. 2 and hands his horse over to him.

No. 9 moves up abreast, and on the offside of, No. 3, and takes his horse.

No. 7 of the right, and the shoeing smith in the left detachment, move up between Nos. 5 and 6 and take their horses.

No. 7 (range-taker) of the left detachment moves up abreast of, and hands his horse over to No. 10.

The signaller hands his horse over to No. 11.

The second serjeant takes charge of the led horses.

The corporal hands his horse over to No. 10 of the right detachment.

10.—SECTION DRILL.

1.—*Formations of the Section*.

NOTE.—In all these formations the two detachments of a sub-section must be kept together, but it does not matter which gun is on the right or left; they are interchangeable.

Line.—The two sub-sections in line, with an interval of 5 yards between sub-sections.

Section column.—The section in column of detachments.

Column of sub-sections.—Sub-sections in column at a distance equal to sub-section frontage, plus 5 yards.

Line of detachment column.—Each detachment in column, at 10 yards interval.

2.—*Diminishing the front.*

" Form Column of Sub-sections."

From line to column of sub-sections. The right sub-section advances; the left sub-section inclines to the right, follows and covers at wheeling distance, plus 5 yards = 20 yards.

" Form Column of Detachments from (the Right, Left, or any named Detachment)."

From line to column of detachments.—The detachment named advances; the other detachment of that sub-section inclines right or left, follows, and covers.

If no flank or detachment is named, the second detachment advances followed by the first, third and fourth in that order.

"Form Column of Detachments."

From column of sub-sections to column of detachments.—The right detachment of the leading sub-section advances; the left detachment inclines to the right, follows and covers.

The rear sub-section acts in like manner, as soon as its front is clear.

3.—*Increasing the front.*

"Form Section."

From column of sub-sections to form section.—The right sub-section continues at the original pace; the left sub-section inclines to the left and moves up at an increased pace into line.

"Form Section."

From column of detachments to form section.—The leading detachment advances; the 2nd detachment inclines to the right, and moves up at an increased pace into line.

The rear sub-section forms sub-section, inclines to the left, and moves up at an increased pace into line, at 5 yards interval from right sub-section.

"Form Section."

From column of route to form section.—Each detachment forms line and thus brings the section into column of detachments. Section is then formed as from column of detachment.

4.—*Moving across country and into action.*

"Form Line of Detachment Column."

From line to line of detachment column.—Each sub-section forms line of detachment column. The right sub-section leader directs; the left sub-section leader inclines to the left until there is an interval of 10 yards between his right detachment and the directing left detachment of the right sub-section.

"Form Line of Detachment Column."

From column of sub-sections to line of detachment column.—Each sub-section forms line of detachment column. The rear sub-section inclines to the left and moves up at an increased pace into line with the leading sub-section at 10 yards interval.

"Form Line of Detachment Column."

From column of detachments to line of detachment column.—Each detachment forms column; the leading detachment advances and directs; the remaining detachments move up into line at an increased pace, the second on the right, the third and fourth on the left of the leading detachment.

5.—*Movements to a flank and rear.*

"Right (Left) Wheel into Line."

From column of sub-sections to form line to a flank.—Each sub-section wheels to the flank named.

From column of detachments to form line to a flank.—Each detachment wheels to the flank named, on completion the left detachment of the right sub-section directs.

"Form Column of Sub-sections (Detachments) to the Right (Left)."
"Sub-sections (Detachments) Right (Left) Wheel."

From line to form column of sub-sections to a flank.—Each sub-section wheels to the flank named.

From line, to form column of detachments to a flank.—Each detachment wheels to the flank named.

The sub-section leader takes post in front of No. 4 of the leading detachment of his sub-section ; the serjeant takes his post in front of No. 4 of the rear detachment, at a distance of 4 feet from serrefile rank of detachment in front.

" Files Right."

From column of detachments, to form line of detachment columns to the right.—As in Section 8 (3) and see note.

" Half Files Right (Left)."

From line of detachment columns, to gain ground to a flank—As in sub-section drill.

" **Sub-sections (Detachments) Right (Left) About Wheel.**"

From line and column of detachments, to go about.—Each sub-section and each detachment wheels about on its own centre.

From line of detachment columns, to go about.—As in sub-section drill.

6.—*From line of detachment column.*

" Form Section."

To form section.—The right sub-section forms sub-section line, and continues to advance.

The left sub-section forms sub-section on the right detachment and closes upon the right sub-section to 5 yards interval.

" From the Right (Left) Form Column of Sub sections."

To form column of sub-sections from a named flank.—Each sub-section forms sub-section.

The right (left) sub-section advances, the other inclines to the right (left) follows and covers in column.

" From the Right (Left) (or any named detachment) Form Column of Detachments."

To form column of detachments.—Each detachment forms line; column of detachments is then formed as from line, each detachment moving by the shortest route to its place in column.

11.—SQUADRON DRILL.

1.—*Formations of the Squadron.*

Line.—The sections in line at 5 yards interval.

Line of section columns.—The sections, each in section column, side by side at such interval that when each section forms line the squadron is in line.

Column of sub-sections.—The sections each in column of sub-sections, at such distance that a wheel of sub-sections to either flank would bring the squadron into line.

Line of detachment columns.—As in section drill. (Plate VII.)

Column of detachments.—Sections, each in column of detachments, in column. Distance between sections is the same as between detachments. (Plate VIII.)

Mass.—The sections, each in section column, side by side at 5 yards interval.

NOTE.—*Inspection Order.*—The sections, in close column of sub-sections, side by side at 5 yards interval, covered off by transport as in Plate IX.

The necessity for manœuvring a Machine Gun Squadron as a single unit is not likely to arise on active service. The above formations are used for purposes of drill and inspections only.

In Squadron Drill the front is diminished and increased, movements made to a flank and rear, and rough and broken ground ridden over, in the same formations and at the same words of command as in Section Drill.

The following points must be noted :—

1. *In line, or line of detachment columns*, the directing section is the centre section, and the directing detachment is the second detachment in the centre section.

2. In forming column from line, the centre section advances, followed by the left, followed by the right section.

" **Detachments to ——— Yards Extend.**"

3. When in line of detachment columns, the interval between detachments may be increased at will. The extension may be made from either flank, or from the directing (*i.e.*, the second) detachment in the centre section.

2.—Formations useful in Squadron Drill not included in Section Drill.

" **Form Line of Section Columns.**"

To form line of section columns.

From line.—Each section forms column of detachments from the right.

From Column.—Each section forms column of detachments; the leading section advances, the second and third sections wheel half right and half left respectively, and move up at an increased pace into line, at an interval of 33 yards.

From Mass.—The centre section advances; the right and left sections wheel half right and half left respectively and extend to 33 yards interval.

" Form Mass."

To form Mass. (Plate X.)

From line.—Each section forms column of detachments, the centre section from the second detachment, the right and left sections from the left and right detachments respectively. The right and left sections then close in upon the centre section to 5 yards interval.

From column.—Each section forms column of detachments. The rear sections then move up into line with the leading section at 5 yards interval, the second section on the left, the third section on the right, of the leading section.

12.—GOING INTO ACTION.

During all preliminary movements, the section will adopt, as far as possible, the formations of the troops with whom it is co-operating.

When the section (or sub-section) officer has reached a point from which he decides to bring his guns into action, the following procedure will be observed as closely as possible:—

(1) The section (or sub-section) officer will explain to his N.C.Os. and men the situation and the special task allotted to the section.

(2) He will go forward accompanied by the signaller, the rangetaker, and an orderly, to reconnoitre and choose the gun positions.

(3) The senior N.C.O. will be left in charge of the sub-section, with instructions :—
  (a) To keep in touch with the officer ;
  (b) To bring the sub-section as far forward as is consistent with reasonable safety ;
  (c) To move the sub-section in the formation best suited to the ground and circumstances.

(4) The section (or sub-section) officer, having chosen the approximate positions for his guns, will signal back for the detachment leaders. The rangetaker will take the ranges and will afterwards be at the disposal of the section officer.

(5) The detachment leaders will join the section officer, leaving No. 1 in charge of the section, with instructions :—
  (a) To keep in touch with the detachment leader.
  (b) To bring up the tripod immediately on receiving a signal.

(6) The section officer will point out the approximate gun positions, allot targets, explain his plan, and indicate probable fire orders, to detachment leaders on the spot.

(7) Detachment leaders will choose the exact positions for guns and signal to No.'s 1.

(8) No.'s 1 will bring up the tripod, closely followed by No.'s 4 with gun. If possible the gun should be mounted under cover, and afterwards moved into position for firing. No.'s 3 will bring up ammunition and find suitable places for themselves in rear, and to flank, of gun positions. Remaining numbers will form a chain of communications between led horses or ammunition dump and guns. No.'s 6 will be at the disposal of the section officer. (Plate XI.)

13.—ACTION.

Subject to the sub-section officer's orders, each detachment leader will control the fire of his own gun. The sub-section leader will not attempt to control the fire of either or both guns directly, but will remain free to watch the general situation, to make and receive reports, to maintain communication with his superior commander and the troops with whom he is co-operating, and to appreciate and conform with any change in the tactical situation.

14.—ADVANCING AND RETIRING AFTER ACTION.

On orders being given to advance, No.'s 1 and 4 will dismount gun, and the hindmost man in the " chain of communication " will immediately advance.

Each of the remaining gun numbers will remain in his position until all numbers in rear of him have arrived at, or at a point in line with, that position, when he will advance

On orders being given to retire, No.'s 1 and 4 will dismount gun and retire. No. 3 will wait until No.'s 1 and 4 are clear and will then advance to the firing point to bring away belt boxes. Each of the remaining numbers will remain in his position until all numbers in front of him have reached that position, or a point in line with it. Sub-sections must invariably be brought in hand again before any change of position is made.

SYMBOLS.

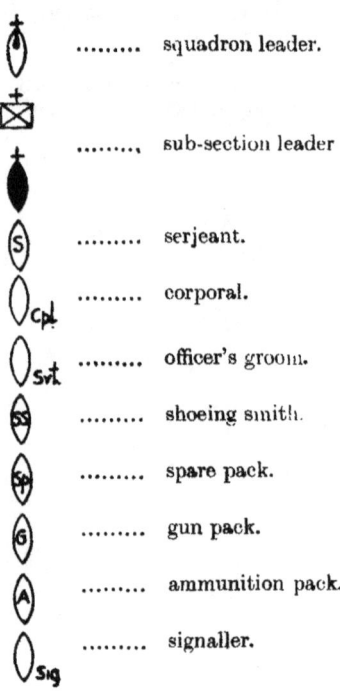

.... squadron leader.

........., sub-section leader

.... serjeant.

.... corporal.

.... officer's groom.

.... shoeing smith.

.... spare pack.

.... gun pack.

.... ammunition pack.

.... signaller.

PLATE I.

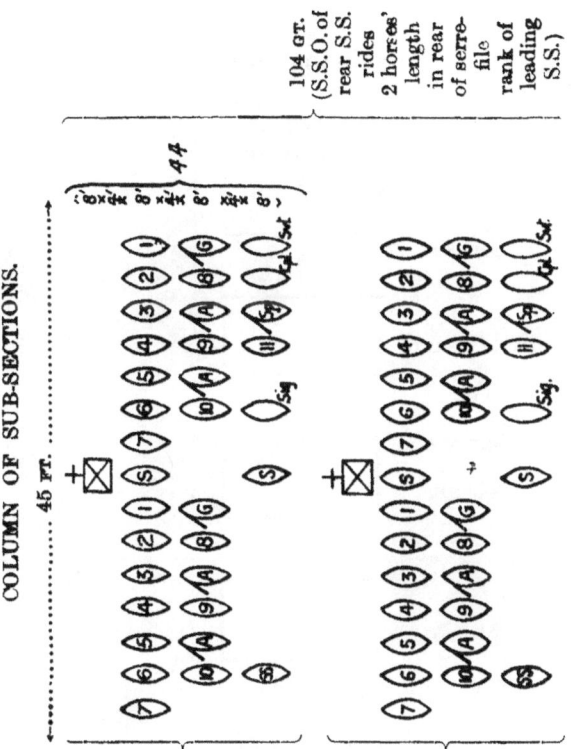

Plate II.

SECTION DRILL

Column of Detachments or Section Column.

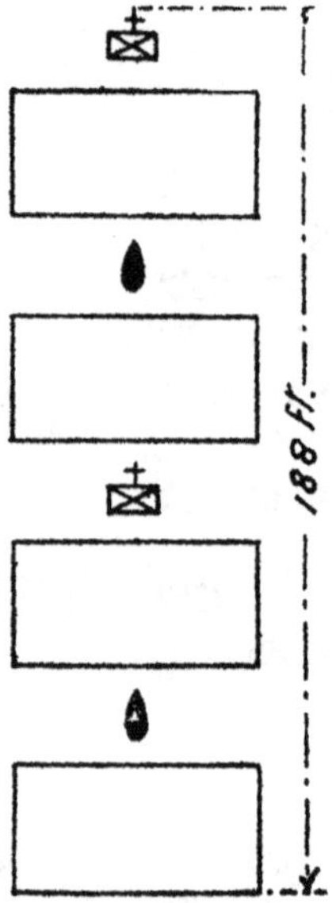

188 Ft.

PLATE III.

SECTION DRILL.

LINE OF DETACHMENT COLUMN.

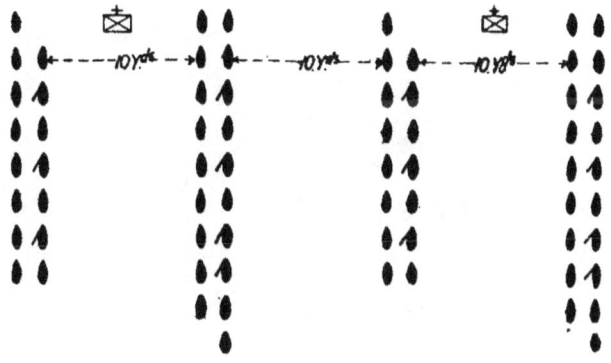

PLATE IV.

SECTION DRILL.

DETACHMENT CONSISTS OF ONE HALF OF A SUB-SECTION.

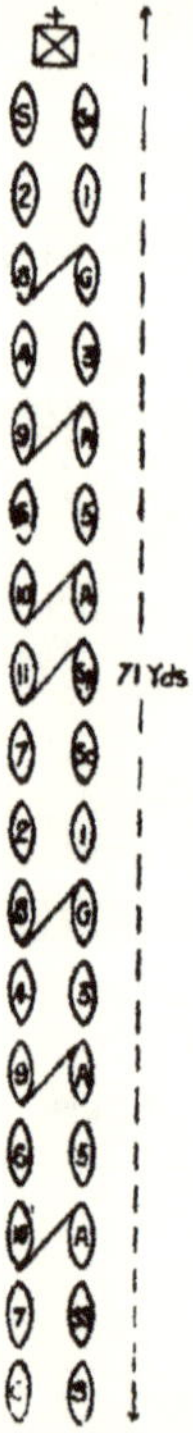

Sub-Section

IN

"Column of Route"

OR

"Advance by Files."

Time to pass a given point.

Walk 4 m.p.h. = 36 secs.

Trot 8 m.p.h. = 18 secs.

Gallop 15 m.p.h. = 9½ secs.

Plate V.

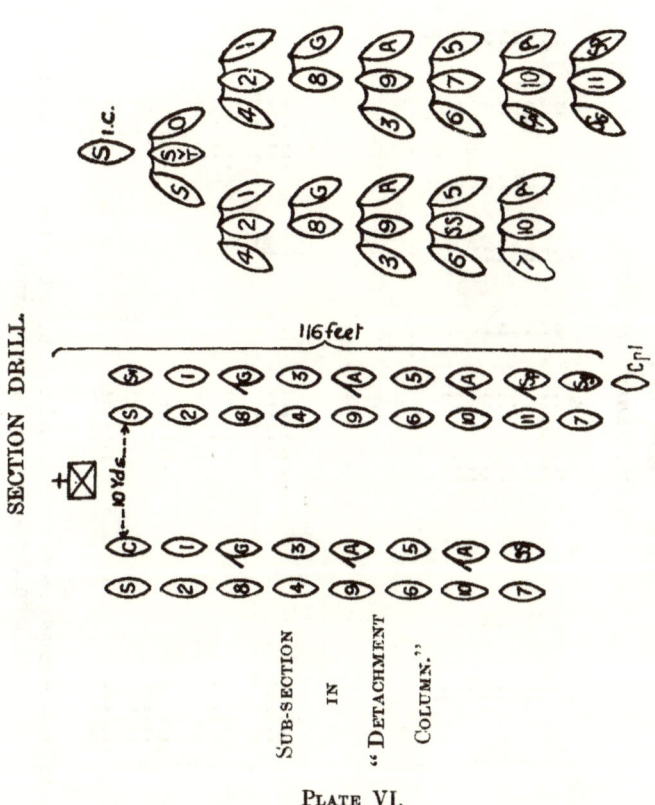

PLATE VI.

32

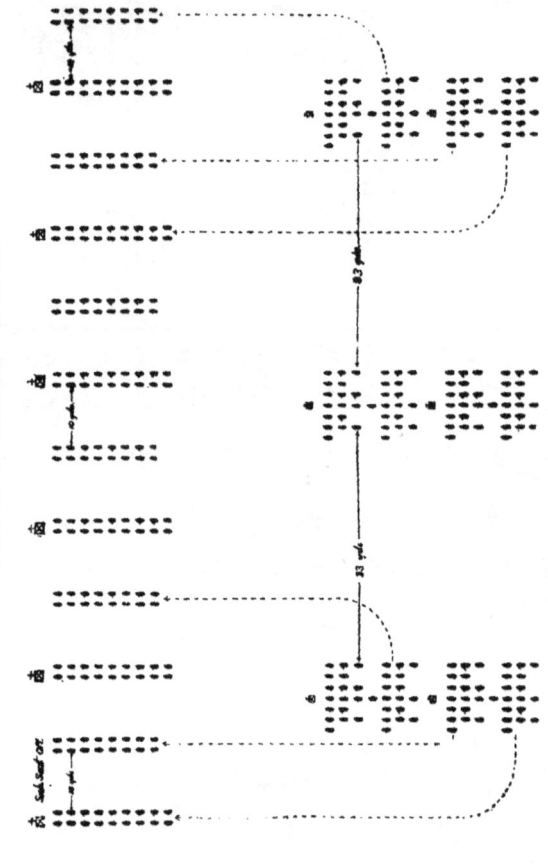

PLATE VII.

SQUADRON DRILL.

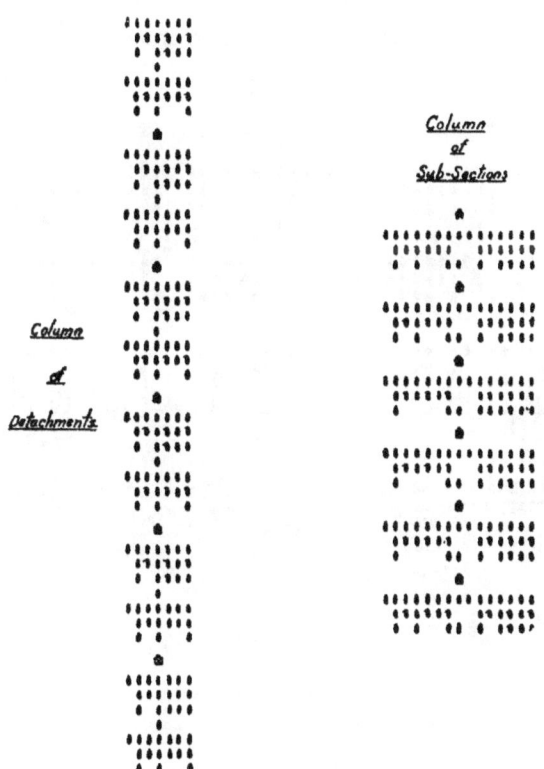

PLATE VIII.

MACHINE-GUN SQUADRON.

Drawn up for Inspection.

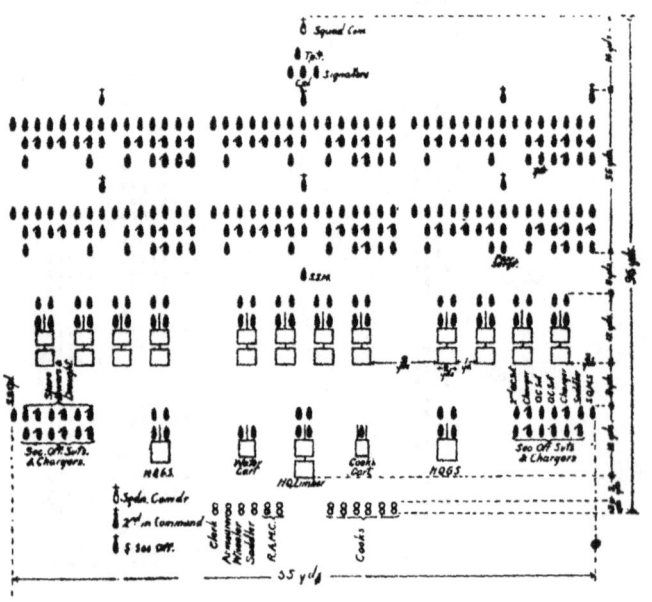

Plate IX.

SQUADRON DRILL.

Mass.

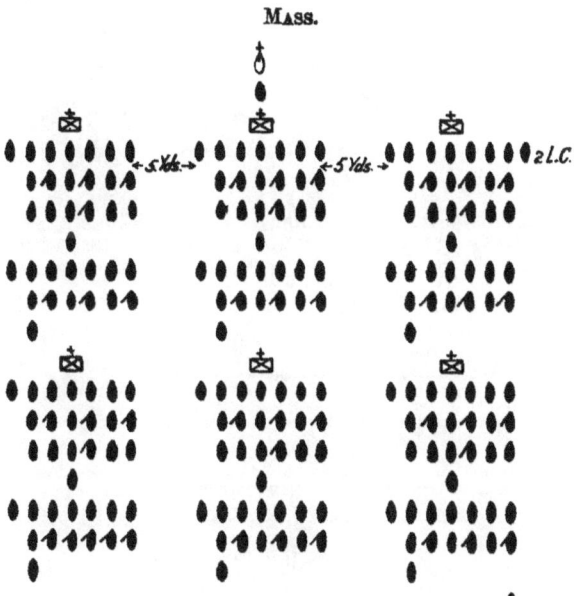

"Section Column" as above with 33 yards interval.

PLATE XI.

A Sub-Section of a Machine Gun Squadron in Action.

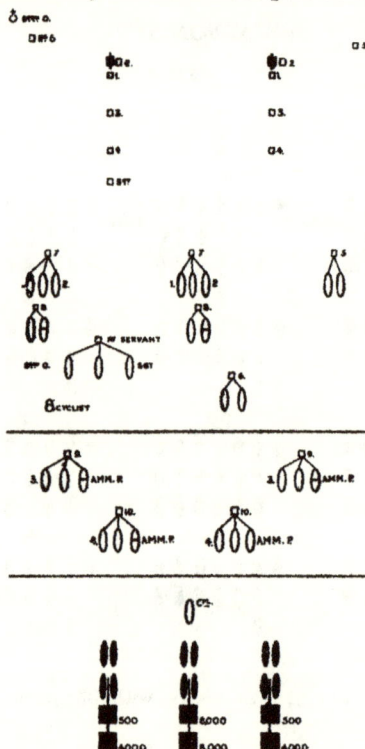

Ο Shoeing smith.
ΟΘ Spare pack.
ΟΘ 2nd servant and charger.

PLATE XI.

40/W.O./4032

FOR OFFICIAL USE ONLY.

Notes and Rules for Barrage Fire with Machine Guns.

MAY, 1917.

Issued by the General Staff.

PRINTED AT MACHINE GUN SCHOOL, MACHINE GUN TRAINING CENTRE,
UNDER THE AUTHORITY OF HIS MAJESTY'S STATIONERY OFFICE.

1917.

Notes and Rules for carrying out Barrage Fire with Machine Guns.

DEFINITIONS.

A barrage of fire produced by machine guns is intended primarily to deny a certain area of ground to the enemy by preventing him crossing one or all of the lines which bound it. A barrage, therefore, may be frontal or flanking (with regard to our own line), or both simultaneously.

Figure I.—**Frontal Barrage.**

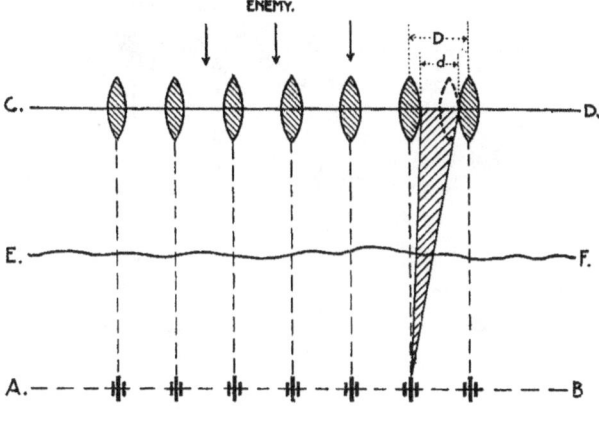

Figure II.—Oblique Barrage.

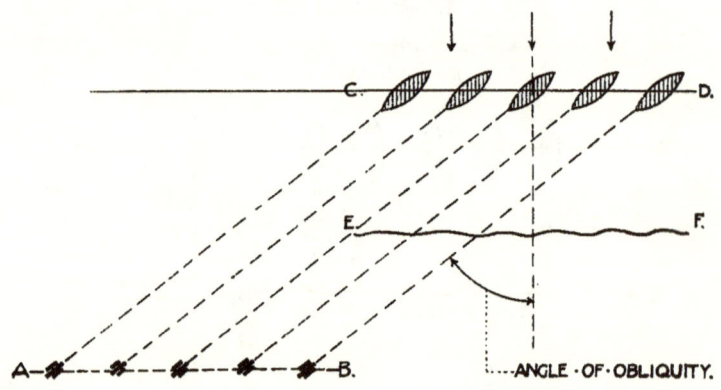

FIGURE III.—**Flank Barrage.**

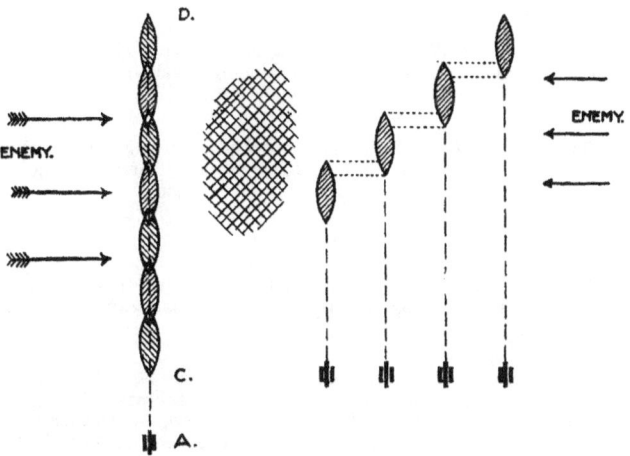

The production and application of the integral parts of a barrage, *i.e.*, of the consecutive zones from the guns engaged, present no new problems at all; the ordinary methods of fire direction for engaging a visible or an invisible target apply with no modification whatever.

GENERAL NOTES.

(a) Limits of front each gun can cover:

There is a LOWER LIMIT and an UPPER LIMIT to the front which each gun can cover in producing a barrage.

The LOWER LIMIT will produce a barrage of high efficacy, comparable in effect to a dense artillery barrage, which should cause (on flat ground) somewhere about 50 per cent. casualties to a hostile body of troops passing through it.

The UPPER LIMIT produces the minimum thickness barrage which can be applied conveniently without gaps.

These two limits really define the opposite ends of a scale between which the machine gun officer can operate, choosing whatever degree of efficacy of barrage he may consider necessary to meet the tactical situation, or to produce the most efficient barrage with the number of guns at his disposal.

(b) As a rough guide, the number of rounds to be fired per burst may be taken as twice the first two figures of the range in yards.

EXAMPLE: Range 2,100 yards; 40-round bursts.

REMARKS.

This type of barrage, produced by using the Upper Limit, might be required, for instance, to stop definitely any attempted enemy counter-attacks, etc.

This type of barrage, might be employed when it is required to deter the enemy from manning parapets, escaping over the open, or making use of any particular area of ground, etc.

RULES.

Rule I.: For Frontal Barrage.

LOWER LIMIT is obtained by multiplying the gradient of descent of the bullet at the range at which the barrage is being produced, by four.

UPPER LIMIT: 70 yards for all ranges.

EXAMPLE: Range is 2,100 yards.
From Table I., Column 3 (vide Infantry Machine Gun Company Training), gradient of descent 1 in 5·5.
Lower Limit = 4 × 5·5 = 22 yards per gun.
Upper Limit = 70 yards per gun.

Rule II.: For Oblique Barrage.

LOWER LIMIT is obtained by multiplying the gradient of descent of the bullet at the range at which the barrage is being produced, by four.

UPPER LIMIT: For all ranges, 70 yards plus 2 yards for each degree of obliquity (*vide* Figure II.) up to a maximum of 150 yards, which must not be exceeded.

EXAMPLE: Range 2,100 yards; degree of obliquity 45°.
From Table I., Column 3 (vide Infantry Machine Gun Company Training), gradient of descent 1 in 5·5.
Lower Limit = 4 × 5·5 = 22 yards per gun.
Upper Limit = 70 + (2 ×· 45) = 70 + 90 = 160.
This is over 150, therefore, 150 yards must be taken.

NOTES.

On Rule I.: For Frontal Barrage.

(a). Traversing must be employed, but there is no advantage gained by searching if only a curtain of fire is required.

(b). If the ground slopes down and away from the guns, both Limits may be increased, and vice versa.

On Rule II.: For Oblique Barrage.

(a). Traversing must be employed, but there is no advantage gained by searching if only a curtain of fire is required.

(b). If the ground slopes down and away from the guns, both Limits may be increased, and vice versa.

RULES.

Rule III.: For Flank Barrage.

In this case, the Limits become the actual differences in sighting elevation to be used on the guns.

LOWER LIMIT is obtained by multiplying the gradient of descent of the bullet at the range at which the barrage is being produced, by four.

UPPER LIMIT: 150 yards for all ranges.

EXAMPLE: Range to nearest zone 2,100 yards.

From Table I., Column 3 (vide Infantry Machine Gun Company Training), gradient of descent 1 in 5·5.

Lower Limit = 4 × 5·5 = 22 yards.

Upper Limit = 150 yards.

i.e., for high efficacy: combined sights with 25 yards differences; for thin but continuous: 150 yards differences.

Rule IV.: Only for Ranges below 1,300 yards.

Use the Upper Limit only, as given in Rules I., II., and III., for all ranges below 1,300 yards.

EXAMPLE: Range 1,200 yards; Frontal Barrage.
Front, per gun, 70 yards.

NOTES.

On Rule III. : For Flank Barrage.

(a). It should be observed that the danger line, through which an enemy has to pass, is much less in thickness in flank than in frontal barrages, as in the latter case, we are dealing with the width of the zone, whereas in the former we are concerned with the depth. Therefore, it takes a much shorter time for a man to pass through, and this emphasises the necessity for continuous fire in flank barrages.

As the number of guns required is not excessive, and others may, therefore, be available, if a high degree of protection is desired, a second barrage should be formed, parallel to the first, with say, 50 yards separating them. The two should not be super-imposed, because, if by reason of any ground formation, or artificial cover, a part of the ground was defiladed in the first barrage, it is probable that such defilading effect would not exist at the same distance from the guns and a little way to a flank. In other words, gaps formed as indicated above in both barrages would probably be staggered, thus rendering the combined barrage continuous throughout its length.

(b). It should be noted that the rules for "combined sights" do not apply to this type of fire, *e.g.*, in this case, differences of 25 yards or 150 yards are permissible.

On Rule IV.

REASON: That although the rule for obtaining the Lower Limit is theoretically correct, it gives large frontages which each gun can cover when the range is below 1,300 yards. The influence of ground (i.e., slight obstacles, undulations, etc.) here becomes so great that it is not advisable to use such large frontages.

Modifications due to Rate of Fire, Speed of Hostile Advance, etc.

(a) The rules given are applicable without alteration to all cases where the ratio—

$$\frac{\text{Rounds Fired by each gun in one minute}}{\text{Speed of enemy advance in yards per minute}}$$ is equal to 4.*

(b) If each gun is firing 300 rounds per minute (about its maximum), the rules then will apply for a speed of advance of about $2\frac{1}{2}$ miles an hour.

(c) If the pace, owing to bad ground, etc., is LESS (than $2\frac{1}{2}$ miles per hour), then each gun can fire fewer rounds per minute and still produce the same degree of efficacy of barrage. (See example).

(d) If you have fixed, beforehand, the number of rounds to be fired by each gun per minute, and if you have estimated the probable speed of advance, the ratio (see No. 1, above), will show you how to modify the rules to meet any particular case. (See example).

---

* This is the figure used for determining the front per gun in the Rules.

Remarks and Examples.

(a) The factor 4, which is given in the rules, is a good "safe" figure to use, and should be used in all cases where there is no time to make further calculations.

(b) *e.g.*, 2½ miles an hour = about 75 yards per minute.

$\frac{300}{75} = 4.$

(c) e.g., Speed of Advance, estimated at not more than 1½ miles an hour, owing to mud, etc., this equals 44 yards per minute.

Number of rounds to be fired by each gun per minute can therefore be found:—

$$\frac{\text{Number of rounds per minute}}{44} = 4.$$

i.e., Number of rounds per minute = 4 × 44 = 176 (or thereabouts).

(d) EXAMPLE.—FRONTAL BARRAGE:

Guns are to fire each 250 rounds per minute. Enemy speed estimated at not more than 1½ miles per hour.

1½ miles per hour = 44 yards per minute.

The ratio becomes $\frac{250}{44} = 5\cdot7$.

Your Lower Limit is now 5·7 times the gradient (instead of 4 times the gradient) for the range.

Your Upper Limit is now $70 \times \frac{5\cdot7}{4} = 100$ yards (instead of 70 yards) for any range.

Printed under the Authority of
His Majesty's Stationery Office,
AT THE MACHINE GUN SCHOOL,
MACHINE GUN TRAINING CENTRE.

www.ingramcontent.com/pod-product-compliance
Lightning Source LLC
Chambersburg PA
CBHW031145160426
43193CB00008B/264